Fragile X Syndrome
a guide for teachers

Fragile X Syndrome
a guide for teachers

SUZANNE SAUNDERS

David Fulton Publishers
London

David Fulton Publishers Ltd
Ormond House, 26–27 Boswell Street, London WC1N 3JZ

www.fultonpublishers.co.uk

First published in Great Britain by David Fulton Publishers 2000
Revised and reissued 2001

Note: The right of Suzanne Saunders to be identified as the author of this work has been asserted by her in accordance with the Copyright, Designs and Patents Act 1988.

British Library Cataloguing in Publication Data
A catalogue record for this book is available from the British Library.

ISBN 1-85346-536-4

Typeset by Textype Typesetters, Cambridge
Printed in Great Britain by The Cromwell Press Ltd, Trowbridge, Wilts.

Contents

Introduction

Fragile X is currently thought to be the most common inherited cause of developmental and learning difficulties.

It is a genetic disorder that gets its name from the appearance of the long arm of the X chromosome where, in people who have the condition, it looks as though there is a fragile piece of material or partial breakage. The condition was not identified and named until the late 1970s when it finally became clear that this break or fragile site on the X chromosome was a cause of learning difficulties in males and that it could be inherited. We now know that girls can also be affected though usually not to the same extent as boys. The next major breakthrough came in 1991 when the gene responsible for the condition was identified. This has enabled scientists to begin to consider why the presence of a faulty gene should cause learning difficulties, though this is not yet fully understood, and also to find out more about the ways in which it is carried and passed on to future generations. It has also enabled them to develop simple and reliable tests for the condition. While much progress has been made in the past ten years, knowledge is still far from complete and many unanswered questions remain.

In the past, it was thought that fragile X might affect as many as one male in every one thousand but more recent studies suggest that it may not be this common. A Mental Health Foundation Briefing Paper in 1999 suggested that it may affect one in 3000 males and one in 6000 females and it is still possible that this figure may be higher that reality. Whatever the exact figures it is still true that fragile X affects a significant number of people and it is still thought to be the most common inherited cause of learning difficulties. (Down Syndrome is the most common genetic cause of learning difficulties but it is not usually thought to be inherited. Despite this it is still not a condition that is well known among the general population and it is likely that many professionals in the fields of social work, health and education who may well come into contact with people who are affected by it, do not have the knowledge, understanding and skills that they would like, to enable them to help these individuals in the best ways possible. However, owing to the fact that awareness of the condition is gradually growing and a simple and reliable test for it is now available, it is likely that many more people with fragile X will have the condition identified in the coming decade and consequently that its profile will be raised.

This book aims to give teachers and others who have contact with children with fragile X an overview of the condition and an understanding of how it affects individuals. It goes on to suggest how those in a teaching role can help them to develop educationally, behaviourally and socially by using strategies and methods best suited to their specific needs.

Chapter 1 briefly describes the medical aspects of fragile X that the teacher will find it helpful to know in order to understand the condition and how it affects an individual. In reality these aspects are extremely complicated but the chapter attempts to give a simplified overview of the medical aspects and to present them in a way that is easily understandable.

How does a teacher recognize a child with fragile X in the class if a formal diagnosis has not been made? What are the signs to look out for that would suggest the presence of fragile X?

It is not easy to answer these questions. There is little in his or her appearance to suggest that a child may have fragile X and while there are characteristics common to those who have the condition, there is huge variability both in terms of which characteristics are displayed by an individual and the degree to which they are evident. However, there are signs or characteristics shared by many of those with fragile X which might enable an informed teacher to suspect that a pupil may have the syndrome, though it should be remembered that as it is a genetic condition, a true diagnosis can only be made by proper genetic analysis.

Chapter 2 looks at the characteristics shared by many people with fragile X. It is important that teachers are aware of the range of symptoms that a child with fragile X may experience or characteristics that he or she may display for three main reasons. The first is to enable a teacher to recognise when a child with whom he or she has contact is displaying signs of having the condition. These initial suspicions may then lead on to an accurate diagnosis being made. The second is to give the teacher a greater understanding of the child and how he or she may be affected by their fragile X. Many people with fragile X display characteristics and behave in ways that others find hard to understand and which appear to be without obvious motive. Some of this behaviour can be explained and perhaps more easily accepted if the teacher has an understanding of how fragile X affects the child and the problems and difficulties that he or she lives with. Thirdly, if a teacher knows what condition a child has, he or she can find out more about that condition and how it might manifest itself and can benefit from existing knowledge about how best to help that child. This enables the teacher to teach that child in ways that have been found to be most effective.

Chapter 3 looks at the ways in which the teacher can make it easier for the child with fragile X to operate within the classroom by creating a suitable environment for him. Certain aspects of the condition make it difficult for the child to behave in ways that may be expected of children in a classroom setting and there are particular situations that can arise in the course of a normal school day that the child may find especially difficult to handle. By understanding these and knowing the individual child, the teacher can structure the environment, plan ahead and make certain allowances that will enable the child to function as well as possible and show the extent of his abilities. This is not to suggest that children with fragile X need to be treated differently from all the other children in the class, indeed they need to learn how to modify their behaviour and how to function in a world that makes few if any allowances for their difficulties. However, if a teacher is faced with a child who clearly has trouble adjusting to the demands of the classroom it makes sense to do everything possible to modify the environment in ways that will help that child to cope in the short term as he gradually learns how to adapt and change in the longer term. If the teacher can be sensitive to situations that are difficult for the child with fragile X to cope with, times when he or she is likely to need extra support and ways of making it easier for him or her to operate despite the difficulties imposed by the condition, life can be made more pleasant for everyone in the class and the child can learn in an environment in which he is most likely to succeed.

Teachers are becoming increasingly aware that all children have their own learning styles and that they are likely to make the best academic progress when they are taught in ways that utilise their learning strengths. While many children are fairly adaptable and will make progress when taught in a variety of ways, some children, particularly those with special educational needs, have less flexibility and are less likely to learn if the teacher is not able to identify the ways in which they learn best and take these into account when teaching them. Owing to the fact that fragile X is relatively 'new' in terms of being identified as a specific condition associated with learning difficulties, there has not been a great amount of research done into the specific learning strengths and weaknesses of children with fragile X or the most effective ways of teaching them. However, research is on-going, knowledge is growing all the time and some facts have emerged that can be of help to the teacher. Chapter 4 looks at the cognitive profile of children with fragile X and identifies their strengths and weaknesses in terms of learning. With this knowledge the teacher can adapt his or her teaching and use strategies that are most likely to be effective in promoting learning.

Of course it is too simplistic to suggest that if a teacher teaches in a certain way success is guaranteed while teaching in another way will bring failure. As with all children, those with fragile X are subject to individual variation and bring their own personalities as well as predispositions to the learning process. However, knowing that certain ways of teaching are likely to be more effective and that certain strategies have been found to be successful with a significant number of other children with the same condition, the teacher has a useful starting point. He or she can go on from there to find out exactly what motivates and helps the child that he or she is teaching and can develop strategies that appear to work best with this individual.

People with fragile X, in common with the vast majority of people, enjoy the company of others and want to make and maintain friendships. It is vital therefore that part of their education is aimed at helping them to behave in ways that other people find acceptable and to relate to others in ways that enable friendships to be made. Many people with fragile X have difficulties in these areas, but they still want to be accepted, liked and approved of. Therefore it is crucial that all those people involved in the education and development of these children work together on the development of behavioural and social skills that will enable the child to achieve the social life that he or she desires. Chapter 5 looks at particular behavioural and social characteristics associated with fragile X and at those which are also common to children with attention deficit hyperactivity disorder and those on the autistic continuum. The possibilities that exist for using medication to control or alleviate some of the symptoms of these conditions are presented, leaving the reader to consider their helpfulness or advisability for children with fragile X. The rest of the chapter is devoted to a consideration of methods that may be used to manage and modify aspects of the behaviour of children with fragile X where they are considered unhelpful to the child and those with whom he mixes.

Finally, in Chapter 6, consideration is given to the families of those children with fragile X and teachers are invited to consider life from their perspective. While these families live with the realities of raising a child who may have severe learning and behavioural difficulties, they must also cope with the fact that the condition is inherited and the implications of this. Parents must accept that they have passed on the condition; other siblings learn that they may be carriers or themselves affected; and there are implications for all future children and the extended family. It is unlike many inherited conditions in that it is possible and indeed not uncommon for a family to carry the faulty gene and pass it through many generations before a child exhibits the full syndrome and is diagnosed. Consequently it can come as a complete surprise to a family that many members may all be affected by it in one way or another. However, once the family has that information, all those affected face many difficult decisions about how they proceed with their lives. This chapter looks at fragile X from the perspective of different family members and tries to bring the reality of their situation to life for the reader.

Within the book, for ease of reading, children with fragile X are referred to as 'he'. This reflects the fact that it is usually boys who are affected by the full syndrome and who exhibit the most severe symptoms. Girls can be severely affected, but this is less common and the majority of girls who are affected have more subtle and less disabling symptoms. Teachers are referred to as 'she' throughout the book, also for ease of reading.

This book endeavours to help teachers and others involved in the education of children with fragile X to do their job with more confidence, knowledge and insight. It provides them with some understanding of the condition and of those children who are affected by it. It suggests ways of providing an environment in which the children can learn, techniques that can be adopted and strategies that are likely to be effective. It goes on to address the topics of behaviour and social development, subjects which are often areas of concern for teachers and others, and finally gives some insight into the lives of families who are affected by the condition.

Through reading this book it is to be hoped that teachers of children with fragile X will be better equipped to teach them in ways that are likely to be effective. It also aims to enable teachers to understand these children and the difficulties that they face in their lives, to appreciate their strengths and to enjoy the unique personality of each one.

CHAPTER 1

What is Fragile X Syndrome?

Introduction

In the first chapter the medical aspects of fragile X are discussed in order to give the reader some background information that will help to understand the condition.

In reality the medical aspects of fragile X are extremely complex and the condition is not yet fully understood. Research continues across the world to discover what happens within the body when a person has fragile X, and knowledge is growing every year. The following information attempts to present current knowledge in a simplified way that will give the non-specialist a clear and understandable overview of the condition.

What causes fragile X syndrome?

It has been stated that fragile X is caused by a fragile site or partial breakage on the tip of the long arm of the X chromosome. In fact, at this point of the chromosome the coils of DNA which make up the genes have become unwrapped but this is so fine that it cannot be seen with an ordinary microscope. So why does this cause a problem? The reasons are actually very complex and still not fully understood. This explanation provides a simplified picture of what happens within the faulty gene.

In 1991, Verkerk *et al.* located the actual gene responsible for fragile X syndrome. They determined that the abnormal appearance of the tip of the chromosome occurs at the site of the gene Fragile X Mental Retardation – 1 (FMR-1). The FMR-1 gene has what may be called a 'housekeeping function', helping other genes to organise their activity. It does this by producing a particular protein that helps other genes in their organisation. Thus it is thought to be a protein carrier and crucial for normal brain development (Freund, 1994). A study by Reiss *et al.* (1991) using magnetic resonance imaging found selective atrophy of a specific brain area in people with fragile X compared to the general population. It was thought that this was the result of the protein deficiency.

In individuals with fragile X, a change exists in the FMR 1 gene. In everybody, the gene contains a repeating chemical sequence of three bases. This is called the CGG repeat. In most people in the population, without fragile X, the gene contains up to approximately 50 repeats. In a person who suffers from fragile X, there are many more repeats of this sequence, possibly thousands. This causes a chemical change within the gene which effectively switches it off. Therefore, the gene no longer performs its usual function of producing a protein, and lack of this protein prevents normal brain development. Thus, fragile X is a condition of a deficiency of the protein coded for by the FMR 1 gene.

The number of CGG repeats also explains why some people obviously carry the fragile X faulty gene but do not suffer from learning disabilities. It has been found that if the number of repeats is between approximately 50 and 200, the individual will be a carrier for the condition and capable of passing it on to their children. They are said to have a pre-mutation. It is only when the number of repeats exceeds approximately 200 that the gene is inactivated and the person suffers the full consequences of the condition.

Inheritance and transmission of fragile X syndrome

It is known that fragile X is an inherited condition and that it can affect many members and generations of a family. However, while it is classified as following a pattern of X-linked inheritance as the mutation occurs on the X chromosome, it is clear that fragile X has an unusual pattern of inheritance and there are anomalies or unusual features of its transmission that are not all fully understood yet.

It is useful to begin, to review some of the basic facts of genetics that explain how most diseases are inherited.

Every individual inherits 46 chromosomes from their parents. These chromosomes are made from genetic material called DNA. The chromosomes are organised into 23 pairs and one of each pair comes from the mother and one from the father. Twenty two of the pairs are called autosomes, and one pair comprises the sex chromosomes. In females, the sex chromosomes consist of two Xs, and in males there is one X and one Y chromosome.

As females have only X chromosomes, they can only pass X chromosomes to their offspring. Males however, having an X and a Y chromosome, can pass on either of these. If they pass on their X chromosome, the resultant child will have two X chromosomes and will be female. If they pass on their Y chromosome, the child will have one X and one Y chromosome and will be male. Therefore it is the male who dictates whether the child is a boy or a girl.

If a mutation occurs on the X chromosome, the resulting condition is said to be X-linked. The fragile X mutation, as we have already seen, occurs on the X chromosome.

Under the normal conditions of X-linked inheritance certain occurrences may be expected:

- A female carrier will not usually display the symptoms of the condition because she will carry it on only one of her X chromosomes and the other 'good' chromosome will cover its effects. She will however be capable of passing it to her children.
- The condition cannot be passed from a man to his son, as he does not pass his X chromosome to him. He will however, pass it to all his daughters as he only has one X chromosome, the affected one, to pass on.
- A female who carries the condition will risk passing it to 50 per cent of her male children, while the other 50 per cent will be unaffected. She will risk 50 per cent of her female children being carriers whilst 50 per cent will be non-carriers.

As we have stated previously, while fragile X conforms broadly to the usual pattern of X-linked inheritance, there are also some unusual features.

The first anomaly concerns the fact that some males may not be affected by fragile X even when it has been passed on to them, but although they may be unaffected themselves, they are still capable of passing carrier status to their daughters.

The second concerns the fact that some women who carry the gene *are* affected by it themselves. They may experience learning, social and behavioural difficulties though the degree to which they are affected varies and they are not usually affected to the same degree as males. Thirdly, the condition tends to get more frequent in families and more severe with the passing of the generations. Finally, while considering the inheritance of fragile X, it is possible for the condition to 'appear' in a family that had no knowledge of its existence in their genes. It is possible for it to be carried through many generations without anyone being aware of it and only when a child displays significant difficulties are tests carried out and the condition diagnosed. This can come as a complete surprise and shock to the family. Genetic counselling following diagnosis is important.

Diagnosing fragile X

In the past, the only method of diagnosing fragile X was by cytogenetic analysis, i.e. examining a person's chromosomes under a microscope. This was fraught with difficulty for several reasons.

It was a major breakthrough therefore when, after the discovery of the gene, a new method of testing was developed. This involves testing a person's DNA and is done from a simple blood test. DNA testing is more sensitive, less time-consuming and more cost-effective than chromosome analysis.

Recent advances which are currently still at a research stage or in their infancy include:

- the development of a test using cells from the cheek, thus avoiding the need to withdraw blood;
- a test involving a prick on the thumb which could produce a few drops of blood to be smeared on a slide and stained to reveal the presence or absence of the protein that is normally made by the FMR 1 gene.

Testing for fragile X can also be done pre-natally by chorionic villus biopsy.

Given that testing for fragile X is now relatively accurate, quick and painless, and that fragile X is known a relatively common inherited cause of learning difficulties, it raises the question of whether some form of screening for the condition should be considered. Modell (1992) describes the findings of a Mencap medical advisory panel workshop which considered the possibility of large scale screening for fragile X. However, Modell states that it was not considered feasible or ethical at that time and that resources should be concentrated on diagnosing children currently known to be at high risk of having the condition, ie. those with learning difficulties, and offering counselling to their families. Slaney *et al.*, (1995), suggested that special school registers could be used to define a population for testing, or a register of all children with Statements of Special Educational Needs. However as greater numbers of children with learning difficulties are being included in mainstream schools, either with or without Statements, these may not be sufficient. Slaney's study in Oxford showed that screening a selection of special school children with learning difficulties in one county was technically feasible, identified previously unidentified cases and was acceptable to families.

To diagnose or not to diagnose?

Some people hold the view that it is almost irrelevant, in educational terms anyway, to spend a lot of time and effort finding out 'what' a child has, when the emphasis should be on looking at the individual with his particular characteristics and helping him to develop the skills and abilities to lead as happy, fulfilling and productive life as possible.

Other people would take the view that knowing exactly what has caused a child to have the difficulties that he experiences is important, not least because this knowledge can enable parents to accept and understand their child's limitations, and can enable professionals to offer the right help in the right way. Needless to say this is not a clear-cut argument and there are no right or wrong answers.

The following points outline the major advantages and possible disadvantages of diagnosis in the case of children with fragile X.

Advantages
- Parents and other family members are often very anxious to know why their child experiences the problems that he does. A diagnosis can bring them this

understanding and help them to accept the problems that the child and the rest of the family have to live with.

- Some parents, especially those whose children are mildly affected, may have been told by doctors that there is nothing wrong with their child. To a parent who knows that there is, apart from being very frustrating, this can lead to the parents feeling that they are the problem and that it is their 'bad' parenting skills that have caused their child to be the way he is. A diagnosis can be a tremendous relief in these circumstances.

- From the child's point of view, he can know that his difficulties stem from a genetic defect that he has acquired through no fault of his own. This may be of immense help to a child who struggles with difficulties without knowing why he experiences them or to the child who erroneously thinks that his problems are somehow his own 'fault'.

- With a diagnosis, many parents feel released to grieve for the child they have not had, and through this, to come to terms with their child as he is. While they have no diagnosis, they live with the hope that the child may be 'cured' or grow out of his problems. Though the diagnosis may cause a loss of that hope, it can lead ultimately to acceptance of the truth and to their concentrating on helping their child with the life that he has.

- Once the child has a diagnosis, knowledge relating to that condition can be offered to the family and to other professionals who work with the child. This might relate to common characteristics of the condition, knowledge about what to expect in the future and knowledge based on experience about the best ways to treat or help or teach the child. In the case of fragile X, knowledge relating to the inheritance aspects of the condition can also be given.

- From the child's point of view, it is good that parents and teachers have access to information that will enable them to be more understanding of the difficulties that he faces in his everyday life.

- Knowledge about the inherited nature of fragile X may lead to other family members being tested and found to have the condition. This may be of particular help to those who only experience mild symptoms, yet nevertheless have struggled with difficulties all their lives without knowing why. This may apply particularly to girls.

- Awareness of the inherited nature of the condition means that family members can have genetic counselling to give them knowledge and support regarding their reproductive options. They can have the advantage of knowing their own status as regards being a carrier of the faulty gene, likely transmission of the condition, and prenatal screening techniques. They can then have professional counselling as they make some of the most difficult and emotionally charged decisions of their lives and live through the consequences of these decisions. While this may not seem like an advantage for those who have to face the horror of making the decisions, they at least have the chance to make informed choices.

- Many support groups or parent groups, formed by people who have personal experience of a specific condition, exist to offer knowledge and support to parents. They can provide the one thing that no other group can offer, namely the support and understanding of people who are in similar circumstances and who can empathise with the particular problems that a family is experiencing. This, coupled with the practical knowledge derived from having lived through it themselves, means that these groups can be of immeasurable help to those who might previously have felt that nobody else really understood what they were going through.

The address of the UK Fragile X Society can be found at the end of this book.

- From the child's point of view a local branch of a support group may offer him the chance to meet other people like him and to mix socially with them. Children with disabilities in our society can be very isolated, often having little or no social life of their own beyond the family. This can get more marked as they approach adolescence when parents may be re-establishing their own lives, getting older themselves and not doing the things that a young person wants to do. The child himself may not want to socialize with his parents, and siblings may be unable or unwilling to include their disabled brother or sister in their social life. (NCH Action for Children, 1994) .
- From the point of view of the child, he may be able to accept himself better by understanding his limitations, and grow in self-esteem by learning new skills, meeting new challenges and making a worthwhile life for himself.

Disadvantages
- Initially at least, parents are likely to feel tremendous guilt stemming from the fact that one of them, always the mother in the case of fragile X, has passed on this condition to their child, however unwittingly. The parent who has actually passed on the gene is obviously likely to feel the most guilt, but as a child is the product of the union of two people, both often feel guilty.
- Grief. Both parents particularly, but also siblings, grandparents and the wider family must face the reality that this child will be disabled for life and may not fulfil the hopes and dreams that are held for him. Support or help for them as they work through this grief is crucial.
- The partner or other members of the family who do not carry the faulty gene may feel resentment at the partner who has brought it into the family. In unresolved cases this can lead tragically to the breakdown of a marriage that might already have been under pressure arising from the strain of raising a child with disabilities.
- The wider family may resent the fact that these particular members have brought a distressing family condition out into the open and made them all aware of it.

While this is totally unreasonable as the condition will have been present but undetected for generations, it is not an uncommon reaction.

- Genetic testing will be undergone by family members providing they give their consent. Having tests and waiting for results will inevitably be extremely stressful for all concerned. Results can also cause friction within families.
- Fear for the future. Learning that your child has an incurable condition that he must live with for life and that other family members will be affected can be terrifying. Parents wonder how they will cope with the consequences of this new knowledge both in the short and long term and how the family unit will manage.
- Fears about how the child will manage in adult life, especially when the parents cannot be there to support him, must also be faced.

Treatment

There is currently no cure for fragile X syndrome. Once a child has been born with the condition it is present for life and the emphasis in treatment is on helping individuals to fulfil their potential despite the handicapping aspects of their condition.

At present, in the absence of a cure, treatment focuses on alleviating the symptoms of fragile X and on educating individuals and their families to understand the condition, minimise their disabilities and make the most of their abilities, so that they can lead as fulfilling lives as possible. With help, improvements can be achieved physically, medically, behaviourally, educationally, psychologically and socially and as we shall see later in this book, there are many treatments, interventions and therapies that offer help to those with fragile X and much that can be done to help them fulfil their potential. However at this point there are two essential features of any treatment regime that must be emphasised.

The first concerns the need always to consider the child with fragile X within the context of their family and social system. While this is true of all children with special needs, it is especially important in the case of children with fragile X because of the inherited nature of the condition and the fact that some other family members may themselves be affected in some way. In helping each child, the needs of the other family members and their ability and desire to be involved in treatment must be taken into consideration. It is they who live with the effects of the syndrome, they who will be at the forefront of any interventions that are carried out, and they who will remain, long after the child has moved into another class or become the client of another professional. Their understanding, cooperation and participation will be crucial factors in the success of any intervention.

Secondly, it must be remembered that no one profession or professional has all the answers. For maximum results, both assessment and intervention need to be multi-professional, with input made by people from a wide variety of disciplines. Fragile X is a complex condition, yet knowledge is limited, with relatively little having been researched or written about it, in this country at least. It requires all professionals to pool their theoretical knowledge with the personal experience of individuals and affected families, for effective intervention programmes to be drawn up. It must also be remembered that while people with fragile X may display many similar behaviours and share certain characteristics as a result of the condition, other aspects of their persona will be unique to them and will require an individual response. Consequently, while professionals can and should extend their knowledge of fragile X to equip themselves better to respond to the needs of fragile X pupils, all responses must be tempered in the light of the needs and abilities of the individual child with whom they are working.

Females with fragile X

Although fragile X is usually associated with males and it is generally true that males are more severely affected by it, the syndrome can and does affect females as well, and some females are severely affected.

Females who carry the faulty gene may be divided into those who are carriers only and those who have the full mutation and can be said to have the condition themselves. (If a female carries the fragile X gene but does not have the full mutation, then the FMR-1 gene mentioned earlier will not have closed down and the essential protein that it makes will still be present.) These females are therefore likely to function intellectually within normal limits. It is only when a female has the full mutation that they are likely to be affected intellectually to some degree. The extent of their learning difficulty will depend on the proportion of the brain cells that fail to express the fragile X protein.

The difficulties experienced by females with fragile X are not dissimilar to some of those experienced by males. Cornish *et al.* (1991) found that girls with fragile X tended to have difficulties in social relationships, specifically having problems with extreme shyness, social withdrawal, and the skills involved in social interactions. She notes that these features extend from childhood into adulthood and can make it hard for the girls to form social relationships at every stage of life. The same study found that in common with boys, girls were relatively more able at verbal skills such as articulation, comprehension and vocabulary than non-verbal skills such as emotion perception, face recognition and visuo-spatial skills. The incidence of girls who suffered from anxiety and depression was also high. These findings indicate that even in the absence of intellectual difficulties, the girl with fragile X can still be very vulnerable at school and support from school counsellors and sympathetic teachers who understand their problems can be crucial to their happiness and social adjustment.

Intellectually, girls in the study reported difficulties in the curriculum areas of physical education and geography, but the most significant difficulty was in the area of arithmetic where they were exceptionally weak. It is important that teachers are aware that girls with fragile X have particular difficulties in the area of arithmetic that is specific to their syndrome rather than a result of lack of interest of effort.

Finally, the study found that girls, in common with boys, had great trouble retaining information in their short-term memory and recalling it to order, particularly if it related to abstract or non-verbal material. This is likely to affect their learning in all areas of the curriculum even when their overall intellectual ability does not appear to be significantly affected. Again, it is important that the particular difficulties of the girls is understood so that extra help can be given to prevent failure in these areas as far as possible.

Owing to the fact that many women who are carriers of fragile X, or who have it themselves do not display significant symptoms, the fact that they are affected is often not diagnosed at all or it is only discovered when the birth of a severely affected male prompts genetic testing throughout a family.

While it is likely to be a great shock to a woman to discover, perhaps in adulthood that they carry or are affected by a genetic condition, for some their shock may also be tempered by a degree of relief. It can be helpful for females who have functioned 'normally' all their lives, to learn that they are affected by fragile X syndrome as it legitimises and explains some of the difficulties that they have been aware of and have struggled with for years, particularly in the area of social functioning and relationships. It may also help some to know that their affected sons who previously did not have a diagnosis have inherited a specific condition that has caused their learning difficulties, and that they are not the way they are because of 'bad parenting', which tragically may have been suggested to them. The diagnosis can also be a catalyst for the women to receive specific help.

However, it must also be remembered that some females exhibit the full effects of the syndrome. These women may be undiagnosed for many years if not all their lives if people who have heard about fragile X erroneously think that it only affects boys. It is crucial that all girls and women receive the recognition and specific help that can aid them in their task of overcoming, accepting or living productively within the limits of their symptoms, however severe or mild.

CHAPTER 2

The Child with Fragile X at School: Characteristics

Introduction

One of the reasons that fragile X was not recognised as a specific syndrome for so long and one of the reasons why it remains under-diagnosed today is that the people who have it are so diverse in terms of the characteristics of the condition that they display and their abilities, disabilities, strengths and weaknesses. No two children with fragile X that the teacher is likely to meet in the classroom will be the same and even when they do display the same characteristics there may be huge differences in the degree to which they display them and the extent to which they affect the child's ability to function.

However, there are specific characteristics associated with fragile X syndrome, some of which will be displayed by a significant number and many of which will be recognisable to those who are familiar with people who have the syndrome. It is not uncommon for teachers, when they become familiar with fragile X or have a child in their class who has it, to think back over their past pupils and recall several who, with hindsight, probably had fragile X. They may also suspect that one or more children whom they currently know or teach may have the condition.

In this chapter I will outline the characteristics of the condition, paying particular attention to those characteristics that are most evident in the school setting or those which are particularly relevant to learning.

Physical characteristics

Appearance

Many boys with fragile X syndrome are extremely good-looking, attractive children and have few, if any, specific characteristics that would lead someone to think that they might have a particular condition. While there *are* certain physical characteristics associated with fragile X, they are subtle and often do not become obvious until the child reaches adolescence or adulthood. Looking at a photo gallery of children under eight or nine, some of whom had fragile X, a person would need to be very familiar with the condition to identify those affected by it. If the same children were to be photographed in adulthood it would be a lot easier to pick out those with the condition as the subtle characteristics of childhood become more pronounced. This lack of easily identifiable physical characteristics make it less likely that the condition will be suspected and therefore tested for early on in a child's life unless the family is known to carry the faulty gene. It is only as other social, behavioural, linguistic and educational difficulties emerge that sufficient pointers may be present for someone to suspect fragile X.

Physical characteristics to look out for which are present in over 70 per cent of children are: a long thin face; prominent, rather sticking out, long ears; flat feet and hyperextensible joints, especially in the fingers (i.e. their joints appear to bend 'too far' or they seem 'double-jointed'); a high, arched palate; low muscle tone (appear rather too 'floppy') and, in boys over eight years of age, large testes (Hagerman and Brunschwig 1991).

Motor skills

In addition to these characteristics that relate to appearance, children with fragile X will often display deficits in both gross and fine motor development which affect the way they move and function at school and every aspect of their daily lives.

Gross motor skills
They are often late in achieving the normal developmental milestones and usually walk late, seldom before two years. When they do walk they have poor balance and are floppy, with a rather loping gait. They usually remain poor at anything requiring balance and appear to find it difficult to move their limbs in a very precise or controlled way.

The reason for their difficulties in this area lies with two specific problems which these boys suffer from. The first is the low muscle tone mentioned earlier which accounts for the 'floppy' appearance. The second is a connective tissue disorder which means that their joints are less well connected, providing a less stable base for movement. This explains why their joints appear hyperextensible and why they often have flat feet, where the arch of the foot has collapsed. These problems also account for the fact that they are prone to scoliosis and other joint disorders.

Fine motor skills
Fine motor functioning is impaired and the boys generally have poor control of their finger and hand muscles. Consequently, handwriting is slow, laborious and untidy, and dressing skills are poor. They also have difficulty with activities involving cutting, manipulating objects and using tools of any sort. This includes

the use of cutlery so they are often messy eaters. Their low muscle tone and joint looseness contribute to these problems alongside a tendency to tactile defensiveness whereby some of the boys appear to find it unpleasant to touch or grasp certain objects. Tactile defensiveness will be discussed later, but suffice it to say here that if a child is finding it unpleasant or overly distracting to have an object such as a pencil in his hand, it is not surprising that he will find it hard to become proficient in using it.

Vision

Boys with fragile X are more likely than the general population to suffer from visual defects particularly a condition called strabismus where the individual cannot make both eyes focus together on an object. Whilst one eye turns as it should, the other turns in a different direction. They are also more likely to suffer from long or short sightedness. All of these conditions can be alleviated or helped by correct assessment and provision of glasses. However, again because of their tactile defensiveness, many boys with fragile X find wearing their glasses very difficult. Consequently they may struggle to focus on their work or to see clearly without their glasses. They may be seen contorting their face to get the best view of something or appearing not to be looking at something when they are in fact struggling to see it as well as possible.

Hearing

As regards hearing and the auditory system, boys with fragile X seem to suffer frequent ear-infections and they risk damage to their hearing if these go undiagnosed and untreated. This propensity may be a result of their connective tissue disorder. They also often appear particularly sensitive to sound, becoming very agitated by and appearing scared by sudden or prolonged loud noises. They frequently cover their ears as if to block out sound. It is hard to know whether they are excessively sensitive to noise in that they hear it more loudly than other people, or whether it is the fact that they find it harder than most people to filter sounds according to their importance. Most people are able to ignore many of the noises that they hear, in order to concentrate on the one that requires their attention. Children with fragile X often find it hard to do this. Consequently they may hear all the noises impinging on their auditory system with equal intensity and cannot ignore those that are currently unimportant. This means that in the classroom they will be hearing the heating system, the lawnmower outside and their neighbour sniffing just as loudly as the teacher's voice. The constant barrage of noise that they may be living with makes it very hard to concentrate on the most important source of noise or the one that they wish to concentrate on. This may explain some of their attention difficulties. Secondly, they may also find it hard to decide which is the most important sound and may choose to pay more attention to the fly buzzing on the window than the teacher talking at the front of the class.

Touch

Children with fragile X syndrome are often described as 'tactile defensive'.
A child who is tactile defensive may:

- dislike being physically touched by another person and avoid, for example, having a cuddle, holding hands, being picked up etc.;
- dislike the carrying out of daily care or hygiene tasks e.g. washing, dressing etc.;
- dislike holding or touching certain objects, especially unfamiliar ones;
- dislike exploratory art activities e.g. clay, paint etc.;
- dislike face to face encounters or maintaining eye-contact.

There are a number of causes, physical and psychological, why a child may exhibit these difficulties and many children with learning difficulties are described as tactile defensive. However while not all boys with fragile X are tactile defensive, many experience it to a certain degree.

Our tactile system has two functions. It acts as protection to keep us safe by recognizing danger e.g. too much pressure, heat, pain, etc. and it enables us to feel so that we can recognise objects without looking at them and discriminate between things that we handle.

It is likely, in the case of children with fragile X, that the protective function of the system overrides its discriminatory function so that even harmless touch sensations are perceived as potentially dangerous and therefore unpleasant.

It must be remembered that of the children who are tactile defensive, each will experience their aversion to touch to a greater or lesser extent. For example, one boy may be extremely reluctant to engage in messy art activities and might throw a tantrum to avoid it. Another may be persuaded by gentle encouragement and may eventually enjoy it when he learns that it does not pose a threat.

The tactile defensive child may try to avoid situations when he knows certain tactile activity may occur or he may simply withdraw when a disliked sensation is felt. Sometimes he can be quite desperate or even aggressive in his efforts to avoid the tactile sensation. In these situations it can be helpful to remember that his tactile system may be identifying the touch sensation as a potential threat that should be avoided. His reaction, rather than being 'naughty' or 'silly' is a very logical response to the information that his tactile system is giving him.

Taste and Smell

Children with fragile X often appear to be hypersensitive to smells and respond to them in a similar way to sound in that they can be totally engaged by a smell and unable to filter it out to concentrate on other things. They often seem very interested in the smell of objects, both food and non-food, and can be seen smelling objects around the classroom. Proximity to the school kitchen can be highly distracting for some children with fragile X as can a strong perfume worn by a member of staff.

Similarly with taste, they often mouth inedible objects and appear to find taste interesting. Schopmeyer and Lowe (1992) suggest that they may find this a 'centering' activity that helps them to concentrate or an activity that calms them down in much the same way that chewing gum helps some people.

The vestibular and proprioceptive systems

These vitally important systems are virtually unheard of outside the relevant professional circles, but an appreciation of their function is essential to an understanding of some of the postural and movement difficulties experienced by children with fragile X and many other motor-impaired children. Together, the vestibular and proprioceptive systems give us our perception of gravity and space and our position, orientation and movement within that space.

The vestibular system

The vestibular system is concerned with our perception of gravity and how we move in relation to it, i.e. whether we are moving or still, how fast we are going and in what direction. It is also concerned with the position and movements of the head. Fisher (1991) describes the functions of the vestibular system as:

- awareness of body position, movement position and movement in space;
- postural tone and equilibrium;
- stabilisation of the eyes in space during head movements.

The receptors for this system are located in the inner ear. The actions of gravity and activity within the inner ear send the relevant messages to the brain.

Schopmeyer and Lowe (1992) explain how a malfunctioning vestibular system can cause problems which range from underactivity to hyperactivity.

If the vestibular system is underfunctioning an individual does not get enough information to his brain about the position and movements of his body against gravity. He will have difficulty in refining and coordinating his movements and in maintaining an upright standing or sitting posture. He will also find it difficult to maintain a calm yet alert state. The child will be constantly moving, perhaps fidgeting in his seat or wandering around the room, in an effort to feed the brain with the information it requires so that it can respond with improved posture and movement. The movement helps to feed the brain with the information it needs to balance the body adequately.

At the other end of the spectrum is the child whose brain receives too much input about posture and movement from the vestibular receptors. This child becomes threatened and fearful that his movements will cause him to fall or lose control of his body. This is sometimes called postural insecurity and at its most extreme even the slightest movement challenge can give rise to real fear akin to how we might feel if we were to contemplate stepping off a tall building. The child is afraid to move but desperately wants to and has learnt over time that he does not always fall. His response is to hold his head and body as still as possible as he moves and he develops a rigidity of movement in an effort to minimise the risk of falling. He may also try to limit his activities to well-known, well practiced movements that he has learnt he can handle safely. He is consequently very reluctant to try new activities.

The child with fragile X may be operating anywhere along the continuum described here. While the symptoms described may occur for a variety of other reasons, it is worth remembering that behaviour which may appear strange and without obvious reason, could well be a child's response to internal feelings that are not apparent to the observer.

The proprioceptive system

The proprioceptive system is concerned with our awareness of our body in space and thus gives us the ability to move in an intentional way and perform movement tasks easily.

The sensory information that makes this possible is generated by the stretching and contracting of our muscles and by the bending, straightening, pulling and compression of the joints between the bones. Consequently, the sensations of the proprioceptive system occur mainly when we are moving, but even when still, the muscles and joints are still sending messages to the brain about our position. This knowledge about where our body is in relation to space enables us to know when we are moving and how far each part of our body moves, without vision. The ability to touch our toes or our nose without looking is possible because of proprioception.

People with poor proprioceptive ability are more clumsy, move more slowly and have impaired body awareness. For example, without adequate proprioception from the hands, information about what the fingers are doing is diminished and tasks such as doing up buttons, using a knife and fork, taking a handkerchief out of a pocket etc. are tremendously difficult. Those affected have to put enormous effort into their movements because, rather than being able to move automatically, they have to rely heavily on their vision and cognitive knowledge about how to move in order to position their body and effect the appropriate movement. Children with fragile X often display such difficulties with fine motor skills.

An understanding of these two sensory systems may help us to understand why children with fragile X perform some of the seemingly strange and to us perhaps meaningless movements that are a feature of the condition.

People whose vestibular and proprioceptive systems do not function very effectively will try to increase the amount of stimulation that the system receives, in an effort to give it sufficient information to work properly. The hand-flapping, rubbing hands together, biting the side of their hands, jumping up and down, and rocking, are movements that can help to increase the information that the brain receives about body position and movement. By carrying out these movements, the child may be trying to compensate for the inadequacy of his vestibular and proprioceptive systems. It is quite possible that these movements may eventually become habitual and provide some comfort for the child, but their origin may be functional and may be the body's intelligent response to a problem. If this conjecture is sound, the answer to reducing the movements, if that is a desired target, is not to expect the child to exercise an enormous amount of self-control to simply stop doing them, but to provide specific help to increase the effectiveness of the vestibular and proprioceptive systems, thus reducing the need for the behaviours.

Sensory integration

Sensory integration is a practice, or some people would call it a therapy, that is stimulating a great deal of interest at the current time, not only among those working with children with fragile X but among those concerned with helping children with a wide variety of difficulties. Within the medical profession the theories behind it are not accepted unreservedly and the therapy itself has not been subjected to the rigorous research or scrutiny that are necessary to 'prove' its effectiveness. While doctors are unlikely to dismiss it completely, the feeling is that the theories are based on speculation about what might happen within the brain and are not backed up by hard scientific evidence. However, other practitioners believe that sensory integration therapy has a great deal to offer those who have difficulty in organising the sensory input that they receive. Schopmeyer and Lowe (1992) believe that the nature of fragile X children's deficits suggests that sensory integration therapy may be a useful part of their occupational therapy programme and state that the experience of some clinicians who have worked in this way with children with fragile X has been positive.

Whereas at present it remains a controversial area, an understanding of the theory of sensory integration is useful. The following summary outlines the work of A. J. Ayres who developed the theories in the USA. It must be remembered that at this time the theories cannot be considered proven accounts of what occurs in the brain but, rather, speculation about what might.

According to Ayres (1979), sensory integration is: 'the organization of the senses for use'. She goes on to explain some of its basic theories as follows.

We are constantly receiving information from our senses about the state and condition of our bodies and of the environment that we are in at any given time. These sensations flow into the brain which must sort and order them, translate them into feelings, knowledge, perceptions etc., organise this new information alongside the information that it already has stored and make decisions about how to proceed or behave next in the light of the new information. For most people this happens in a split second and we are not consciously aware of the brain's activity. Ayres likens the brain integrating the senses that it receives to a policeman directing traffic. If the sensations flow in a well-organised or integrated manner, the traffic flows swiftly and well. If sensory integration is poor, it is more like a rush-hour traffic jam in a large city – hundreds of cars trying to progress along their chosen route but getting jammed, progressing in fits and starts and getting re-routed etc.

Sensory integration is essential to living a human life. It begins in the womb as the growing baby senses the movements of its mother and moves itself around. Once born, an enormous amount of sensory integration must occur in order for the baby to learn how to roll over, sit up and crawl. Childhood play provides a vehicle for a great deal more sensory integration as the child learns how to use sensory information effectively to provide information about the world. As we grow up we are constantly refining and fine-tuning our skills of sensory integration. Sensory integration is not something that we either have or do not have. Like most other skills, some people are better at it than others, either because they were born with a greater ability for it, or because they have practised and honed their skills in a particular area, e.g. Ayres suggests that a dancer develops good integration of his or her body in space and acting against gravity, while an artist develops good integration of eye and hand sensations. Ayres also suggests that people who are calm and happy usually have good sensory integration and we are all familiar with people to whom life is easy and who appear to do everything they attempt successfully and well with seemingly little effort. However, most of us function adequately with an average level of skill in this area and never give a thought to our ability to integrate our senses. While every child is born with the capacity for sensory integration it is only by using his body, interacting with the world and adapting to its many challenges during childhood that this adequate sensory integration develops.

The theory goes on to postulate that children who have poor sensory integration skills have greater difficulty functioning in the world. Their brain is not integrating the sensations that it receives as well as it might, and this results in the child having to make a great deal more effort in order to move and interact with the environment, and even when he puts in this effort, he will be less successful than other children in a range of skills.

He may be clumsy, stumble frequently when walking or running, have difficulty playing with toys that require manipulation and find dressing and eating hard. He may be poor at listening and unresponsive to the spoken word even though his hearing is adequate. He may miss details in pictures, be poor at puzzles, find it hard to colour in between lines or cut around a shape even though his eyesight is technically normal. When he goes to school he is likely to have difficulty with the tasks involved in classroom life such as doing up shoes, moving around in a confined space, following instructions, taking care of possessions, paying attention to the teacher in a room full of distractions etc. This is in addition to the difficulties he will encounter in learning and sports activities. For him every task is more difficult and therefore less rewarding and satisfying. He is therefore less likely to be keen to participate in such activities and more likely to be thought lazy or uninterested by adults. Many children with poor sensory integration develop behaviour problems as a result of their experience of life as being hard work and often unrewarding, with their best efforts being less good than the efforts of others and adults not appreciating the difficulties that they experience. They may display hyperactive behaviour such as rushing round the room, being unable to settle, knocking things and stumbling as they go. It is not because they want to do this particularly, but because the excess activity is a reaction to the bombardment of sensory information that they cannot organise properly.

If these theories are accepted they provide an explanation that enables teachers and others to understand and appreciate some of the difficulties experienced by their pupils who have problems in this area. Sensory integration therapy (detailed descriptions of which are outside the scope of this book) aims to help the child learn how to order and organise sensory information better in order to alleviate some of his difficulties.

Doubtless the controversy surrounding this therapy will continue and hopefully further research will continue to shed light on the topic. In the meantime it must not be forgotten that other more traditional responses to the problem behaviours that have been described continue to be used, often with a high degree of success.

Speech and language characteristics

Children with fragile X syndrome are often late talkers and it is not uncommon for them to reach two and a half or three years before the beginnings of speech are heard. This delay in language development persists throughout their childhood. However, it is usually commensurate with their general level of retardation and the speech they eventually produce is around the level of their cognitive functioning. Additionally, their articulation of words often resembles that of a younger child with many of the immaturities of speech common in young children.

It is in terms of their intelligibility and speech production that children with fragile X show a distinct pattern. The majority are hard to understand unless the listener knows the child well. They can usually pronounce single words or very short phrases intelligibly but when they begin to put sentences together, intelligibility is reduced and the longer the sentence or period of speech, the more likely it is that the child will become hard to understand. Dykens *et al.* (1994) summarise the findings on speech production and describe the rhythm of speech as not being smooth, even and fluent, as it would be with a normally developing child, but coming in short, rapid bursts, followed by long pauses, reminiscent of bursts of machine gun fire. There are lots of repetitions of sounds, words or phrases which makes their speech sound 'cluttered', and their intonation is unusual, with emphasis or stress being put on what seem to be the wrong words in the sentence. They also seem to find it hard to coordinate their breathing and speech in the way that most people do without thinking and often sound breathless and need to take breaths frequently in the middle of sentences. Boys with fragile X also find it hard to be appropriately quiet and tend towards constant speech, often as a monologue to themselves. The more stressed they are, the more intense their self-directed conversation becomes. Schopmeyer and Lowe (1992) suggest that it is almost as though they are using it as a mechanism for self-calming, to maintain self-control or to reduce their anxiety.

When it comes to using language for conversational purposes, boys with fragile X often have a surprisingly good knowledge and use of vocabulary, especially in areas of particular interest for them. They do, however, show evidence of echolalia (repeating some or all of the previous speaker's speech), have difficulties sequencing their ideas correctly in a conversation, retrieving some of the words that they want to use and taking turns appropriately. Additionally, they find it hard to stay on a topic of conversation and show evidence of tangential thinking where their answer to a question may bear little or no obvious relation to the question asked. However, it is often possible to see a link between question and answer if the speaker knows the child well and is familiar with other aspects of his life or his particular interests.

The most common characteristic of boys with fragile X, however, is perseveration. Sudhalter (1992) describes this as exhibited by 90 per cent of boys. Speech perseveration is the repetition of single words or phrases over and over again. She suggests that it may be caused by: an inability to locate the next word in a sentence or the next idea in a conversation; an impulsiveness which causes them to state whatever is on their mind regardless of its relevance; or it may be a symptom of anxiety, or a lack of familiarity with conventional word patterns. Sudhalter's later research (1995) found that perseverative language was reduced, though not eliminated, when the speaker did not look at or focus attention on the child and when the environment was quiet and calm. This would lend credence to the theory that this trait is caused or exacerbated by anxiety, at least to some extent. A final feature of their conversational ability which is not related to language or speech production, but is nevertheless a very distinctive characteristic of conversation with a large proportion of people with fragile X syndrome, is their inability or extreme reluctance to make eye-contact or hold the gaze of the speaker. This gaze avoidance will be discussed in more detail shortly.

Behavioural characteristics

Needless to say, people with fragile X will display a huge range of behaviours, only some of which will be a direct result of their condition. Some may be common among people or children with learning difficulties, though less common in the rest of the population; some may be due to their efforts to compensate for or alleviate difficulties that they experience; and others may be learned responses that the child has adopted consciously or unconsciously to help him function more successfully in his life.

The behaviours outlined here are those that have been observed to be specific to males of all ages with fragile X.

Hagerman and Brunschwig (1991) summarise the most common behavioural characteristics as gaze avoidance; speech preserveration; hand flapping; imitation skills; tactile defensiveness; tantrums, physical aggression, and hyperactivity with short attention span.

Gaze avoidance

The most common characteristic, displayed by 91 per cent of children and 95 per cent of adults with the condition, is that of gaze avoidance. It often takes the form of turning the whole head and even upper body away from the speaker. Gaze avoidance is a common feature of children on the autistic spectrum and this may well be one reason why children with fragile X are often thought to suffer from autism. However, Cohen *et al.* (1988) studied the social gaze of a variety of groups of people with learning disabilities and discovered that while children with autism avoided the gaze of all people without discriminating between them, children with fragile X did discriminate in the degree of their avoidance between strangers and their parents, showing a greater degree of avoidance in the company of strangers. This would suggest a higher degree of social awareness on the part of the boys with fragile X. Teachers also report that pupils in their classes become increasingly able to meet their gaze as they become more familiar with them (Saunders 1997).

It would also appear that boys with fragile X do actually desire social contact despite the message given to the contrary by their gaze avoidance. People who are familiar with a child with fragile X will confirm that if they do not try to establish eye-contact, but look elsewhere, the child will make periodic glances towards them and will be able to hold that gaze for varying lengths of time. They also frequently show desire to be in close proximity with known and trusted adults though they might withdraw if they feel any pressure to make more contact than that which the child himself has initiated.

If, as parents and teachers report, children with fragile X do actually enjoy and seek some level of social contact, it is interesting to speculate as to why this gaze avoidance may occur. One possibility is that it is a form of hypersensitivity, similar to that which causes touch avoidance. The child perceives the gaze acutely and is overwhelmed by the resulting sensations. Turning away is perhaps an attempt to reduce the intensity of their response which is unsettling or even unpleasant for them.

Speech perseveration

Hagerman and Brunschwig (1991) cite perseveration of speech as the next most common behavioural characteristic with 92 per cent of children and 94 per cent of adults displaying it.

Hand flapping

Although hand flapping is seen in other people with learning difficulties, it is displayed by over 80 per cent of people with fragile X. One reason for this, along with hand biting which is displayed by 60 per cent, could be that the person is trying to perform a repetitive activity to enable him to cut out or reduce external stimuli which are becoming overwhelming. It could also be an attempt to compensate for the inadequacy of his vestibular and proprioceptive systems by providing the brain with additional movement information. It could also be a response to the child's increasing anxiety.

Tactile defensiveness

This is cited as the next most common behavioural characteristic, displayed by 80 per cent of people with the condition.

Imitation skills

These are noted in 77 per cent of people with fragile X and can be seen by their often extraordinary ability to impersonate other people (often unwittingly), to copy accents that they have heard and to imitate the habits or mannerisms of familiar people. In the classroom these skills can be harnessed to teach the child a whole range of skills through practical example.

Tantrums

These are exhibited by 75 per cent of children and adults, though the number and intensity of the tantrums usually reduces as the child becomes an adult. These outbursts, that often appear to be without obvious cause or triggered by unavoidable events in everyday life, are frequently cited by parents and teachers as being particularly difficult to handle and control. They can, though do not always, include aggression to themselves, other people and/or the immediate environment. However, it is possible to reduce them, partly by finding out what triggers them and controlling the environment to cut down on the occurrences that are likely to provoke an outburst and partly by helping the child to manage his own reactions in a more acceptable way.   These and other aspects of behaviour will be discussed more fully in Chapter 5.

Physical aggression

This is displayed by 60 per cent of people with fragile X. From what we have learned so far about the difficulties experienced by people with fragile X in terms of physical and sensory deficits, it is not difficult to understand that their daily living involves problems and struggles that most of us cannot comprehend. Add this to a range of learning difficulties and the fact that many of the people with whom they come into contact may lack understanding of their problems and unwittingly make unrealistic demands on them, it is not surprising that frustration and anger may result. When a person has limited ability and difficulty understanding and expressing emotions, physical aggression is a common consequence.

Saunders (1996) suggests that many of the behavioural difficulties of boys with fragile X appear to be related to their unusual ways of processing sensory information and their inability to inhibit any sensory input that they receive. This leads to their becoming over-stimulated by their environment, which can result either in tantrums or in the child withdrawing and seeking refuge in very focused or ritualistic behaviours. Whatever explanations may be put forward, it has certainly been found that certain conditions are more conducive to calm, controlled behaviour than others, and these will be discussed later.

Hyperactivity and a short attention span

While Hagerman and Brunschwig only report 18 per cent of people with fragile X as displaying these, amongst parents and teachers they are cited more frequently. Saunders (1997) states that 63 per cent of teachers in a recent study found their pupil with fragile X to be hyperactive and 56 per cent to have impaired attention control. Perhaps they are particularly significant behaviours in a classroom setting where the ability to be fairly static and to concentrate are important to the smooth running of the class and to the learning process.

Intellectual and cognitive characteristics

In males with fragile X the range of cognitive functioning is very wide and whilst 20 per cent may have IQs within the normal range, approximately 80 per cent have a degree of learning difficulty. (Mazzocco and O'Connor 1993). Hagerman and Sobesky (1989), estimate that 30 per cent of males with fragile X have severe or profound learning difficulties, 50 to 60 per cent fall in the range of those with moderate learning difficulties and 10 to 20 per cent are functioning in the normal or near normal range.

Cognitive and learning strengths

It is not suggested that people with fragile X have particular outstanding gifts in these areas, but that given their whole learning profile, they have some relative strengths.

These include:

- *Long-term memory*, especially when it is factual information and in subjects that interest them.
- *Visual memory*, e.g. remembering directions to a place and the things that they pass on the way. Visual clues often elicit a desired response that was not forthcoming from verbal prompts.
- *Imitation.* They learn a lot from those around them and enjoy copying. They can learn a lot of practical and concrete skills through imitation.
- *Verbal Imitation.* They can repeat words and phrases that they hear, especially if the words have an interesting sound, e.g. Abergavenny. They are also good at copying accents and tones of voice and will often unwittingly make excellent impersonations of other people.
- *Verbal Skills.* These include articulation, vocabulary, comprehension and reasoning. They often have a particularly good vocabulary relative to their general level of functioning, especially in areas of interest, where they can acquire and use quite difficult subject-specific vocabulary and terminology.
- Greater skills in *simultaneous* processing than in sequential processing. This means that they are better at remembering or understanding or doing the whole of something e.g. a whole word or a whole picture or a whole task, rather than building it up step by step. They find it hard to put separate parts together in sequence to form a whole and tend to see each part as being a separate entity.
- *Practical skills.* They tend to enjoy and respond well to practical tasks especially those that involve physical activity such as moving around, using simple equipment, making things etc. Teachers often report that they can perform the practical tasks of daily living better than their intellectual capacity would suggest.

Cognitive and learning weaknesses include:

- *Abstract thinking and reasoning.* They find this particularly difficult and are often distracted in their thinking by attending to irrelevant aspects of the task. Because of their difficulties in abstract thinking they find mathematics particularly difficult especially beyond simple computation.
- *Short-term memory.* This is particularly poor and they have difficulty holding information in their mind and recalling it shortly afterwards. However the same child who cannot remember what he did today may have detailed recall of it once it is committed to long-term memory. It would appear that short-term memory is better when the child is calm and relaxed, and when there are contextual clues to help him access the information.
- *Sequencing.* This includes: motor planning, e.g. deciding on the sequence of steps to undertake to complete a task; building up parts in a particular order to complete a whole, e.g. building up phonic sounds to make a word; and following a set of instructions.
- *Verbal Response and Recall.* They have great difficulty responding verbally to questions, even when they know the answer. However, they often respond correctly to a question asked to another pupil. They also find it hard to talk about what they know when they are asked, but may talk about it in detail at a later date, when they initiate the conversation.
- *Selecting and concentrating on the most important aspects of a task* whilst ignoring the less relevant ones.
- *Problem solving.* This demands the ability to bring to mind a number of possible alternative solutions. The child with fragile X will have problems with the recall of options and with the ability to mentally 'try out' these options. They tend to get fixated on one, possibly irrelevant, aspect and find it hard to reject it.
- *Tasks involving fine motor skills.* As the demonstration of knowledge in so many areas in education is dependent on performing some task such as writing, lack of skill in this area impinges on almost every subject. Most children with fragile X find writing hard and are rarely proficient at it.

Conclusion

In this chapter we have discussed the characteristics that appear to be features of fragile X syndrome. Some of these same characteristics may be seen individually in the general population and more may be seen in people with other learning difficulties. However, research and experience have shown that people with fragile X are more likely to demonstrate some or perhaps all of these tendencies to a greater or lesser extent. Of course, each child with fragile X is different and is a product of his own individual personality, skills and abilities; the environment in which he has grown up; his experience of life; and the help that he has received from parents and others. All of these will combine with the specific effects of the fragile X gene to create a unique person. However, when parents or teachers, or others who are familiar with boys who have fragile X discuss the boys, there are many similarities and they report problems, characteristics or experiences that all are familiar with. It would appear that despite differences, particularly in the degree to which a child displays a particular characteristic, possession of the fragile X gene does have a fairly strong influence on a child.

If a child who has not been diagnosed with a specific condition shows a significant number of the characteristics described in this chapter, it would be reasonable to suspect fragile X.

It is not possible to diagnose fragile X without a proper blood test and any testing and diagnosis should always be accompanied by appropriate counselling. It must be remembered that a diagnosis of fragile X, because of its inherited nature, has repercussions for the whole family. Therefore the suggestion of fragile X should not be made lightly, and if a teacher and school feel that it is appropriate to suggest to a parent that their child might have fragile X, provision for the necessary tests and genetic counselling should be made as soon as possible if the family choose to proceed with them. The whole family are likely to need information, support and practical help if they have to come to terms with the fact that it is not just one child but the whole family who have a problem that will affect them all in different ways.

CHAPTER 3

Creating a Conducive Classroom Environment

Characteristics of the child in the classroom

While all children with fragile X are different they also share many characteristics and display many similar traits as a result of the fragile X gene. Similarly, in the classroom, there is a range of specific behaviours that are common to many children with fragile X and which we therefore conclude are influenced by their condition.

Some of these behaviours are likely to make it difficult for the child with fragile X to operate within a traditional classroom setting even though they may be understandable with greater knowledge of the condition. While the boys may not necessarily be 'naughty', they can present management problems for the teacher. It is not uncommon for class teachers to find that managing some of their behaviour within the context of the whole class presents the greatest challenge when teaching a child with fragile X. However, with an understanding of why the boys behave as they do on occasion and a knowledge of the activities and events that are likely to be difficult for them to cope with, it is possible to organise the environment in such a way as to prevent conditions that cause them difficulties and thereby to avoid triggering some of the less desirable behaviours. While undesirable behaviour may not be completely eliminated in this way, it is likely that it can be significantly reduced.

We now go on to consider the characteristics or behaviours that teachers report to be common among pupils with fragile X in a classroom setting. We will analyse these behaviours more fully and make suggestions about how the teacher can create an environment in which the child is most likely to function successfully and thereby enable him to achieve the best results.

Overactivity or hyperactivity

Children with fragile X tend to be constantly on the move in the classroom, rushing from one task to another and failing to settle in one place for long. They find it hard to sit still long enough to complete a work task and when they are seated they wriggle around on their seat, shift position frequently and appear to find it hard to get comfortable. They leave their seat and wander round the room frequently and often need reminding to return to their work. While it can be very disruptive in a classroom to have a child who behaves in this way, it is important to consider possible reasons for the behaviour.

First, it is possible that the child's vestibular system will be impaired (see Chapter 2) and his brain will not be receiving sufficient information about gravity as it is acting on his body, his position in space, and his movements. The constant physical movement, particularly the wriggling and the shifting of position may be the child's unconscious response to this as he tries to feed the brain with the information that it needs to enable him to balance and move effectively. Second, an impaired ability to integrate and make sense of all the sensory information that he is receiving may result in the child being bombarded by sensory information that overwhelms him, makes it hard for him to concentrate, and makes it difficult for him to settle to his task. Consequently he appears restless, unable to apply himself to his work and unwilling to stay in one place.

Teachers find that it is not successful to demand or expect their pupils with fragile X to stay still or remain in their desk for lengthy periods. Indeed with an understanding of the difficulties that they face, this may not be a realistic expectation.

Instead, in order to maintain a smooth running classroom, teachers must recognise the child's need to leave his seat and move around more frequently than most other children and build opportunities for it into the routines of the lesson or the day.

For example, the child with fragile X could:

- help by giving out equipment or paper to the whole class;
- collect the things he needs for his work himself;
- bring his work to the teacher to be checked at an agreed stage;
- deliver a note to another class;
- go to fetch a book from the library;
- sharpen the pencils;
- wash the mugs;
- sort out some apparatus, etc.

It will also be useful to have one or more activities of a practical nature that the child can go to or get out when he has completed the work that is required of him.

In a nursery or infant classroom there are many such activities available, but these often diminish as the children get older. To go to a place where he can use, for example, story tapes, construction kits, practical maths equipment etc. all provide the child with a reason to move around the room and a physical, open-ended task that he can participate in at his own level. These activities can also be used as rewards when the child has completed a required task.

While a successful classroom routine for the child with fragile X will incorporate opportunities for moving round the classroom, it is important to gradually build up the child's ability to remain seated or concentrate on a task for a period of time. The ability to remain seated for a sufficient length of time to complete a sedentary task or to remain in one place while he and the class receive instructions or undertake a short listening activity is crucial to his cognitive development, his functioning, (especially as he gets older) and also crucial for the smooth running of the class. Therefore, while understanding the difficulties under which he functions, it is important that the child be helped over time, to reduce his need to rush or wander round, and to increase the length of time that he is able to settle physically and remain seated.

It is important that the expectation for 'on-seat' behaviour is realistic and it may only be appropriate to expect it to be maintained for a few minutes at the start. However long is decided, the child should know clearly, right from the start, how long he must remain seated. It is not helpful to give him an open-ended task that could take an indefinite amount of time to complete; rather, give him a task with clear-cut requirements where he knows how much he has to do, when it is ended and how far through the task he is at any point.

If the child is engaged in a more open-ended activity e.g. painting or craft, singing or a group activity etc. it can be useful to have a timer that the child can help to set, so that he can see how the time is going and know that he can have a period moving around when the time is up. The child with fragile X is likely to respond well to the practical and very visual nature of this.

The actual seat that the child with fragile X uses can also have an effect on his ability to sit still. Often he will move constantly in his chair, squirming and fidgeting around, sliding off, and seeming to find it hard to get comfortable. To help, a chair that allows the child to have as much of his body in contact with it as possible is needed. A chair with a back and sides is helpful, and this may be padded with cushions or wedges so that the child fits snugly into it and can feel that a large proportion of his body is touching it. Fur strips could be stuck to the chair to indicate where the child should sit, or a rubber mat could be added to reduce the slipperiness of the seat. There are commercially available beanbag chairs that boys with fragile X find comfortable and which are worth considering for certain times in the day. However, they may not be the best chairs for encouraging the children to develop good posture as they are rather conducive to slouching. A compromise might be adopted whereby the beanbag chair is used for the periods when he is required to sit at a desk and apply himself to a specific work task. He can then concentrate harder on his work as he is not distracted by feelings of discomfort. However, for other times, a chair that provides maximum body contact but encourages the child to use his muscles to develop a good sitting position is required. It is particularly important that children with fragile X are helped to develop a good sitting posture as, due to their low muscle tone and connective tissue disorder, they are prone to curvatures of the spine.

Distractibility

Children with fragile X find it hard to concentrate on a task, losing concentration quickly in both individual and group situations and finding it very difficult, or needing help, to regain concentration. They can be distracted by the simplest of things: within themselves, e.g. discomfort; in their immediate environment, e.g. the equipment they are using to do a task; or in the wider environment, e.g. noise in the classroom or outside.

It has been noted that children with fragile X are extremely sensitive to any sensory input and also that they find it very hard to filter out the sensory input that is not relevant to the current situation. The average classroom is a busy, active and very stimulating place. Apart from the teacher talking there are the noises, however subtle, of the other children, scraping chairs, the central heating, a fan, the computer, the clock, the next-door class, PE in the Hall, the lawnmower outside, traffic etc. etc. Apart from the work-sheet that he is trying to complete he can also see the movements and expressions of the other children, the posters on the wall, the mobiles hanging from the ceiling, the paintings drying, the hamster, his watch and clothes, the LSA who is working with another child, the birds outside and the trees blowing in the wind. Distracting smells may well include the smell of dinner cooking, the scent of the teacher, the paint-pots in the corner, the play-dough, the soap he just washed his hands with and the ever-present smell of school disinfectant.

The child may also be aware of the feel of his clothes on his body, especially a tight waist-band or the stiff collar of a shirt, the feel of the pencil in his hand, the chair underneath him, the grooves in the desk and the pressure of his glasses on his nose.

With all these sensations possibly competing for the child's attention at any point in time, and all experienced equally keenly, it is hardly surprising that he finds it difficult to concentrate on his work for long, however hard he may try.

The answer to helping the child with fragile X is to provide a classroom or a space within the classroom that is as distraction-free as possible. It is obviously not practical or possible to completely remove all sources of distraction, especially as the rest of the class may enjoy and benefit from the stimulation provided. However it should be possible in most classes to create an area that is as distraction-free as possible where the child with fragile X can go for work sessions.

This could be done by:

- putting portable display screens around his desk when they are needed;
- providing a desk between the wall and the back of a book-case or set of shelves;
- hanging a curtain from a runner on the ceiling and pulling it to create a private space etc. etc.

If it is available, an adjoining or nearby separate room, or a large cupboard or alcove that could be kept distraction-free could also be used. In most schools, space, especially storage space, is at a premium, and an immediate reaction to this suggestion would be to deny the existence of such an area. However, many schools also have storage cupboards that harbour the accumulation of decades of papers, equipment, books, worksheets etc. that nobody has used for years. Perhaps some clearing out, re-shelving and amalgamating of resources could produce a useable space. Once established, it is highly likely that a distraction-free area would prove invaluable for many children, not just those with fragile X, as it is becoming common practice to provide such a space for pupils with a range of attention deficits.

Short attention span and impulsivity

Linked to both of the above is a short attention span which makes it hard for boys with fragile X to spend long on an activity or to complete tasks that require sustained attention. They will often rush through a piece of work to get it finished in the shortest possible time and will be resistant to returning to it to improve it afterwards. It is not uncommon for the teacher to set work for the individual or the whole class that she estimates will take perhaps 15 minutes, only to find the child with fragile X has 'finished' in two or three minutes, having made a very poor job of it.

Boys with fragile X are also impulsive in a classroom setting. They act first and think afterwards, tending to want to do something as soon as it comes into their head and being unable to wait for an object or an event that they are anticipating. Consequently they appear to rush at things without sufficient thought, make careless mistakes, and seldom give a task the care it needs to complete it well.

The creation of a distraction-free area, in which he can work as described above, is likely to help the child to concentrate longer. More specific techniques to increase attention span and reduce impulsivity will be discussed in the next chapter.

Need for routine and dislike of change

Boys with fragile X respond best when their day is highly structured. They like to know what is going to happen next, what is going to happen during the course of the day, and what will be expected of them. They like each day to follow a pattern that they are familiar with, and for each day to adhere to the expected routine. It would appear that anxiety is reduced significantly when they can operate within the safety of the known routine and they themselves are more likely to be able to maintain a calm, relaxed demeanour. Therefore, in order to create a learning environment that is helpful for the child with fragile X, the teacher should work out a daily routine that will meet the needs of all the pupils in the class, teach it to the pupils, particularly to the pupil with fragile X, and endeavour to follow it as closely as possible every day.

This may sound as though I am recommending a rather regimented, inflexible approach to teaching. However, there is an extent to which many if not most children, particularly those with learning difficulties, appreciate a structured day where they feel secure in the knowledge that they know what is going to happen.

The degree of structure that I am suggesting as being helpful for the child with fragile X may not be a great deal more than would be present anyway within many classrooms.

An example of a structured day for a primary school aged pupil with fragile X

> *Arrival* – same routine of coming in, taking coat off, greeting staff and pupils, settling to a task that has been left on his desk.
> *Registration* – child with fragile X has the special task of taking the register to the office.
> *Making up of personal Schedule Board* to show the activities of the day.
> *Work session* – individual task, followed by time of own chosen activity when the teacher-directed task is complete.
> *Drink* – all children sit on carpet while another child hands drinks round.
> *Break* – same routine of toilet, putting on coat and going outside.
> *Work session* – working as part of a group, but with individual work at each child's level included. Free choice afterwards.
> *Lunch* – accompanied by LSA as he goes into hall, chooses food, seats himself, eats and clears away.
> *Work session* –practical activity e.g. Art, music, PE etc. Same activity on each day of the week e.g. Monday = Art etc.
> *Clearing up.*
> *Story/Poetry time/Reflecting* on the day as a class or group.
> *Home routine* – accompanied out of classroom to taxi.

It can be seen that this schedule is not significantly different to that adopted in many special schools or ordinary primary schools. There is an extent to which it does not matter what the routine is provided that the child knows it and it is fairly consistently adhered to each day. Schedule Boards provide one method of helping a child with fragile X to come to terms with the routine of the day.

Schedule boards

These are simple, often home-made boards that can be used to show the events of the day in the correct sequence. Use of these boards has been found to be particularly useful for children with fragile X, who respond well to knowing what is going to happen to them that day.

At its simplest, the board could show just one photograph of an object or an activity that the child is going to do next. For example, the teacher chooses a photo of the water-tray and puts it on the board. It remains on the board all the time the child is expected to play with the water, and at the end of the activity, the child takes it down, to signify the end of that activity.

As the child progresses, three photos could be used. The water-tray, a photo of a cup of drink, and a tray of cutting and sticking equipment. The child is then shown the photos and it is explained that he will play with the water, then have a drink and then do some cutting and sticking. As each activity is finished, the child can remove the photo. To start with, it may be appropriate to just cover the events of the day to break-time. As the child develops, he may be able to follow the schedule up to lunch-time, or to the end of the day.

Progressions can be to replace the photos with symbols that represent the activities, and later still, as the child learns to read, to use words.

Many boys with fragile X are helped greatly by these boards and they can become lifelines to them to help them see their way through a possibly complicated and anxiety-provoking day. The boards help them to feel secure in the knowledge that they know what is going to be expected of them, they can see what is going to happen next and they can remove the activities that have already gone, thus helping them to see how much of the day is left.

Arrival at school

It is worth giving special consideration to the management of this time of day because it can be a particularly difficult time for children with fragile X and therefore a difficult time for the teacher to manage. This might be because they have unfinished business from home that may be dominating their thoughts or because the journey has been traumatic for some reason or because they had to walk through a crowd of other children to reach their classroom or for a host of other reasons. However, with forethought, the teacher can be aware of the potential difficulty of this time and plan sensitively, to help the child and maintain order.

On arrival, it is helpful if the child can be met from the taxi or bus and accompanied to his class using the same route through the school. The child probably needs to take off his coat and hang it on his own peg and put any possessions that he has brought with him into his own drawer, desk or locker. It is helpful for him to go about these tasks in a routine way before, or on, entering the class. The observance of this routine will help him to make the transition between journey and school and help him to relax and see the school day as safe and non-threatening. However, something as simple as another child having erroneously put their coat on his peg could cause great distress. If the child has found the first part of his morning difficult, he is likely to have a raised level of anxiety so that when he enters the classroom he is in a state of arousal. At this time the classroom needs to be calming and predictable, with no great demands being made on the child. He is likely to need a few minutes to wander round, to check that all is as it should be and that everything is in order. It is not worth making any demands on him for these first few minutes as he will find it hard to settle or concentrate until he feels at ease. After this, he needs to know what he is expected to do, and where he is expected to do it. It is probably not a good time for him to work with others or participate in a group. Rather, a relatively 'safe' task that he feels secure with is likely to help him to become calm and relaxed so that he is in the best frame of mind to go on to greater challenges. The jigsaw puzzle is one example of a range of suitable activities that might be used. It is not necessary for it to be the same puzzle, though he is likely to have a favourite that he may be rewarded with after doing the one the teacher has put out. The exact nature of the task is less important than the fact that he knows where to go and what to do, and that he is capable of the task given to him.

Coping with change

It is not possible to avoid any disruption at all to a child's routine and it is important that the child with fragile X is helped to come to terms with and accept change. In a school setting and later on in the wider world, unexpected events and unforeseen happenings are often the norm rather than the exception, and predictable routines cannot always be adhered to. It is also desirable that they can enjoy special events such as outings and parties and other surprises of a pleasurable nature.

Therefore, while the teacher needs to understand the child with fragile X's need and preference for routine, she also needs to find ways of helping him to cope with change and supporting him through changes in routine that may be traumatic for him.

Techniques that have been found to help in this include:

- preparing the child well in advance for known events. For example, if a class trip is planned, it can be helpful to talk about it well in advance, discuss where the class is going, how they will get there, what they will do when they are there etc. The child can then feel that he is not going into an unknown situation, but one where he knows what to expect and which he is looking forward to.

- having a clear, simple calendar on which to put special events and marking the days off as they pass so that the child can see the events coming nearer and see when they are going to happen.

- using the schedule board to 'flag up' changes in routine. Not all changes are known about well in advance. Sometimes a particular event may only be known about at the beginning of the day. Many children who find a schedule board useful are able to cope with a change that has been incorporated into their day on their board. This gives them prior warning and also helps them to see exactly when the change will occur. They seem to find the presence of the board so reassuring that they can follow its guidance even through change.

- providing the support of a trusted member of staff during a time of change. If something unexpected suddenly happens or a change has to occur at the last minute or, despite careful preparations, the child is anxious or fearful about a change, having a trusted member of staff to be with them and talk them through it and give reassurance can be helpful. Often a learning support assistant or nursery nurse can fulfill this role as the teacher may need to be involved with the whole class and not be able to give the level of support needed to just one child.

- finding out the exact nature of the fear. For some children with fragile X, the fact that change is happening is enough to raise their level of anxiety to a pitch that they find hard to cope with. For others it may be a specific aspect of the event that causes fear. For example, a child may be looking forward to going to the zoo, but be scared about going in the school mini-bus. He may not mind the school nurse or the room used for examinations, but may hate having to take his clothes off. Knowing the exact source of the anxiety may enable the situation to be changed somewhat to avoid it.

Anxiety in social settings

As already discussed, boys with fragile X are very reluctant to meet the gaze of other adults or children or to have physical contact with them. However, they do appear to be very interested in the life of the class and may be the first to point out someone else's misbehaviour or something new or different within the room.

They appear to be generally anxious and ill at ease in large group or whole class situations, particularly if they think they are going to be called upon to answer questions or make a specific contribution. Behaviours such as hand-flapping, hand biting and tactile defensiveness, all common signs of stress or anxiety, are often worse at these times.

They often get very upset when other children are naughty, get into trouble, or have arguments with each other. They appear to become agitated if the teacher has cause to get angry, raise her voice or deliver punishments, even if the displeasure is not aimed at them. Their own efforts to stop two children arguing or to halt what they perceive as bad behaviour, can be as disruptive in the classroom as the original problem.

Conditions that reduce the boys' anxiety are those where calmness, order and relative quiet are maintained. They operate best in a well-ordered class where conflict is rare, either between pupils or between pupils and staff, and where a fairly constant level of noise can be maintained. It is not that they cannot tolerate noise around them, rather that they dislike sudden or very loud noise or disturbance that might lead to unexpected upset or trouble. Sudden loud noises, such as a door slamming forcefully or a pile of books falling on the floor, can be so disturbing for a child with fragile X that he may be unable to regain his equilibrium for the rest of the session or even longer.

The ideal teacher for a child with fragile X would be one who maintains good control over the behaviour of the class, who creates an ordered and calm classroom environment and who approaches the child in a calm, non-threatening way. A lively, extrovert or volatile teacher who might be very good at rousing and stimulating some pupils, might need to change her approach when dealing with boys with fragile X. This is not to say that a teacher cannot have fun with a boy with fragile X, indeed, they usually have a well-developed sense of humour, enjoy jokes and respond well to the use of humour in their learning. However, the child is likely to be sufficiently relaxed to appreciate and respond to humour and fun within the context of an environment that they feel to be safe and secure.

Maintaining a quiet, calm atmosphere in the classroom can do a great deal to prevent the child with fragile X becoming over-stimulated and resorting to undesirable behaviour. Most teachers of these boys develop strategies for calming them as they become aroused and defusing situations that might lead to trouble.

Habitual motor behaviours

Hand-flapping, hand biting and rocking are very common behaviours in the classroom and they tend to increase when the child feels under pressure or is anxious.

On the one hand these behaviours can be seen as stimulatory activities, undertaken to increase information to the brain about the movement of the body. They are also quite common behaviours undertaken by people who are over-stimulated by a situation and who are trying to block out the flood of sensation that they find too much to handle. They do this by retreating into stereotypical, ritualistic behaviour. Whatever the reason for them in the case of the child with fragile X, it would appear that the best way to reduce them is to reduce the child's anxiety. Attempts to focus on the behaviours themselves and to expect the child to eliminate them by exercising self-control are largely unsuccessful. Instead, techniques that help the child to become calm and relaxed and to divert his attention to other activities will meet with more success. In terms of classroom environment, a well-ordered, calm environment with a consistent routine that does not provoke anxiety in the child, is likely to help.

Tantrums or outbursts

A large number of boys with fragile X have periodic tantrums or outbursts which can involve aggression to themselves, aspects of the environment or other people. It is also true that some boys with fragile X can be oppositional at times. The causes of their outbursts are many and varied and will depend on the child. However, from what we know about boys with fragile X it is unlikely that their tantrums or outbursts are provoked by a desire to behave badly, hurt others or be destructive, as they are by nature usually children who prefer order and harmony.

Teachers report that most outbursts occur as a result of:

● sudden noise or upset in the classroom;
● other children becoming disruptive or upset;
● a change in routine;
● having to be in a large, busy, crowded place, eg. school dining hall;
● not being able to do what they want to do at that time.
(Saunders 1997)

This knowledge may help a teacher adapt circumstances or negotiate with the child to alleviate his need to throw a tantrum.

A Personal space

It has been found that children with fragile X respond well to the provision of a personal space in the classroom that they can retreat to, or be encouraged to use, when they are highly stressed and when they feel in danger of losing control. This is not a place for 'time out' as it is commonly understood, i.e. a place where the child is put as a punishment for bad behaviour. Instead, it is a place where the child can escape from the pressures that he perceives or the excess stimulation or whatever it is that is causing his anxiety level to rise. It may be that the teacher guides the child to this place when she sees the signs that he is becoming over-aroused and a tantrum is likely. Once there, the child can be helped to calm down by being offered items or activities that help him feel secure and which reduce his arousal level, or by sitting quietly by himself until he can regain his composure. As he progresses, he can be encouraged to initiate the use of his space and to go there whenever he feels it necessary, in order to control his emotions. Many teachers have found that making space in their classroom for such an area, even if it is simply the child's own desk, placed in a quiet corner out of the way of the general hubbub of the class, has reduced the number of tantrums that their pupil with fragile X has displayed. Encouraging the child to use the area for himself prompts him to take more responsibility for the management of his own behaviour, which has to be a worthwhile long-term aim. If it is used well this system can help the child to become increasingly aware of what is happening both inside himself and in his immediate environment at those times when he finds it difficult to cope behaviourally. Going to his own area then gives him a strategy to enable him to maintain his own equilibrium.

While it is not possible or reasonable to modify the child's environment to the extent where he is never over-stimulated or provoked to the point of a tantrum, it is helpful in the interests of the smooth running of the class to minimise situations where over-stimulation is likely to occur, or to think how the child with fragile X may be helped to cope in a less disruptive manner with the events that he finds difficult to accommodate or accept. If the teacher is aware of the reasons behind his outbursts and the things that are likely to trigger them, she can choose the degree to which she structures the classroom and the day in a way that will be most likely to help the child to behave appropriately.

Conclusion. Creating a conducive classroom environment

The first part of this chapter shows that there is much the classroom teacher can do in terms of organising the classroom environment, planning the day and developing a flexible attitude to some aspects of behaviour, to make life easier for the child with fragile X. It is useful to summarise the aspects of classroom environment that are likely to be under the control of the class teacher and which she can manipulate in order to enable her to get the best from her pupil.

Children with fragile X are likely to function best when:

- the general atmosphere within the class is one of order, calm and quiet. This is not to suggest that pupils have to work in silence, or that a general hum of activity is undesirable. Rather, that sudden noise and unexpected interruptions and distractions be kept to a minimum.
- there is a clear, consistent routine that the child can know, understand and be helped to follow. Children with fragile X function best within a highly structured and predictable setting so that they can feel secure in the knowledge that they know what is going to happen and what is going to be expected of them.
- the room is as free from distractions as possible. This includes visual, auditory and other sensory distractions. It also includes the distraction of unexpected events such as people coming into the room or children having therapy sessions in the classroom etc. While it may not be desirable or possible to eliminate all distractions, it is helpful for the teacher to appreciate just how disturbing they will be to a child with fragile X and the degree of support the child will need to

maintain concentration through distractions or resume concentration afterwards.

- the child has his own space within the room that he can retreat to when necessary. This space is not a place that the child is sent to in a judgmental way, as a punishment, but a quiet place where he can feel safe, reduce his level of anxiety and be free from the pressures or conditions that have caused his distress. Used sensitively, the provision of such a space can be used to encourage the child to take responsibility for controlling his own behaviour and avoiding the need for tantrums.

- the other members of the class function in a reasonably harmonious manner. It has already been noted that children with fragile X often become extremely upset by lack of harmony amongst their peers, even if they are not involved in the dispute and are not getting reprimanded themselves. While it will not be possible to avoid disputes arising in a classroom, when class groups are being considered, it is worth giving some thought to the nature of the children who are to be in the same group as the child with fragile X and if possible, avoiding placing them with a lot of children who are known to have particular difficulties with behaviour and relationships.

- there is sufficient flexibility within the organisation of the class to allow times when the child can leave his seat and move around the room. While it may be felt that staying at a desk for designated periods is an important skill to cultivate and that a child who is allowed to wander at will around the room is distracting to other pupils and sets them a bad example, it must be remembered that children with fragile X do find it particularly difficult to stay in their seat for long periods. Teachers find it unsuccessful to demand the same level of 'on-seat' behaviour from their pupils with fragile X as they do from their other pupils and discover that allowing a certain amount of wandering or finding legitimate reasons for them to move around the room is more realistic. They can then work at increasing the expectation of sitting for longer, in a gradual way.

In a classroom where the conditions discussed in this chapter are created and maintained as far as possible, the child with fragile X has the best opportunities for maintaining a calm, equable demeanour and functioning in a way that will enable him to learn to the best of his abilities.

I would not wish to suggest that the onus is entirely on the teacher to create a classroom environment that will accommodate the child and his problems and remove the need for him to learn how to function in other more traditional or challenging settings. Even if it were possible it would not be desirable. Indeed it is crucial that the child is helped to develop strategies to function in a wide range of settings and to enjoy a wide range of experiences if he is to enjoy a full and satisfying life. I would suggest however that it is a wise teacher who appreciates the need to achieve a balance between accommodating the child's behaviour by adapting the environment to help him to function as well as possible and changing the child's behaviour so that he can transfer the good or successful strategies that he has learnt in the classroom to other environments that he finds himself in. How the balance is achieved will depend on a number of things, including the age of the child, his level of cognitive functioning and the stage of development that he has already attained. At the start, it may be necessary to manipulate the environment to a large extent in the ways that have been suggested. Later it may be appropriate to expect the child to be more flexible and more skilled at adapting to less conducive settings and to exert a greater degree of control over his behaviour.

CHAPTER 4

Teaching Strategies

Planning a programme

Early intervention

It is generally recognised that children with learning difficulties benefit from an early intervention programme which focuses on their general developmental needs as young children, their specific needs as defined by any known condition and the particular difficulties that they experience as individuals. Children with fragile X are no different and the earlier that an integrated programme of intervention can begin, with parents and professionals working together, the better the outcome is likely to be.

It should be remembered that unless there is a known history of fragile X in the family, it is unlikely that the child will have been diagnosed as having the condition before they reach school age. This is partly because the condition is still, at present, relatively unknown to the public at large and to local health and medical workers, and partly because the characteristics displayed by the child in the early years, though a cause for concern, might suggest one of a range of problems and do not necessarily point to fragile X. As fragile X becomes more well-known, as is likely in the coming years, it is possible that more children will be diagnosed earlier and an informed programme to help the child can be put into place in the preschool years. This can only be beneficial.

Working together with parents and professionals

Fragile X is a condition that affects every aspect of a child's life. While it is true that he has learning difficulties, he also has problems that cause difficulties in other areas and a range of needs that cannot be met by one person. Therefore it is crucial that parents and all the professionals who are involved in the development of the child have contact with each other, are aware of interventions that are being initiated in other areas and plan their own input in the light of the other things taking place in the life of the child and his family. Programmes should be coordinated to support and complement each other.

Components of a programme

When a child is diagnosed as having fragile X, there are particular aspects that should be included in an intervention programme.

Educationally the child will need to be placed in a setting where there are:

- staff who understand his condition and the particular needs that may arise because of it;
- sufficient staff to provide the support that he may need in the classroom;
- staff with the knowledge and expertise to plan and implement a programme of learning appropriate to his level of development;
- other children who can fulfill his social needs.

This may be in a mainstream or a special school depending on the severity of the child's difficulties and the location of the necessary resources.

On the medical side it is important to check for vision defects as early as possible as these are common in children with fragile X. They are also prone to frequent ear infections which can begin in babyhood, as early as six months. If these are missed or go untreated, hearing loss can result. Unfortunately this occurs quite frequently.

The earlier that appropriate action is taken to compensate for these and any other sensory defects the less likely it is that additional difficulties will occur as a result of the child living and growing up with the original undiagnosed problem. For example, language delay, which is likely in children with fragile X, may be greatly exacerbated by poor hearing; balance can be affected when inner-ear damage occurs; and the child's ability to explore his environment and manipulate objects can be impaired by poor vision.

Most children with fragile X experience language delay, so speech therapy is a crucial part of any programme. This is likely to focus on the specific difficulties that they experience in terms of speech production, as well as development of their language skills. The speech therapist may also work on eating skills if these are particularly poor for the child's age, and might consider the introduction of a simple augmentative communication system so that the child can begin to make his needs and feelings known to those around him, in the absence of speech. For example, the child may be taught some manual signs from a signing system such as Makaton, or he may be introduced to the idea of pointing to pictures or symbols that have been placed on a board in order to choose an activity or make his needs known.

Most children with fragile X have delayed gross and fine motor development and when they do achieve the normal motor milestones the quality and efficacy of their movements are reduced. This is a result of two problems common to children with fragile X, namely a connective tissue disorder and hypotonia (low muscle tone). Physiotherapy is therefore an important part of the programme. It may focus on posture, body awareness, balance and coordination. It may also concentrate on improving hand function so that the child can be helped to explore objects and materials in the environment more easily. In the early years, physical and sensory exploration of the environment is crucial for learning development and should be encouraged and facilitated as much as possible.

Occupational therapy is also desirable to help reduce sensory defensiveness and improve sensory awareness, to improve attention and concentration, and to help the child to function most effectively in the tasks of daily living.

Another crucial aspect involves working with parents to help them understand and come to terms with the nature of their child's difficulties and the reasons for his delayed development. This might include information about fragile X syndrome and the characteristics that their child might display as a result of having the condition. It should also include discussion about the difficulties that their child may face in his daily life and the best ways of helping him. The task of parenting is constant whereas at best a therapist is only likely to work with a child once or twice each week. Therefore the more parents are helped to carry on the work of the therapists in helping the child to function effectively in everyday life, the better.

Parents of children with fragile X frequently cite their child's behaviour as one of their chief concerns and help to understand and manage this is crucial. They can be advised about how to structure the environment, prevent over-stimulation, manage trantrums appropriately and use therapeutic calming techniques. The earlier that good behavioural patterns can be established, the less likely it is that undesirable ones will become entrenched. This will make life more pleasant for the whole family and parents are likely to feel more confident in their ability to handle and address behaviour problems should they arise later.

Finally, it is crucial that a programme for a child with fragile X includes time to interact socially with other children in a non-specialist setting. Children with fragile X usually enjoy the company of other children and are interested in them. They are excellent mimics who observe those around them and can learn a great deal about how to behave by imitating others. The opportunity to learn from children who are developing normally and who do not experience specific difficulties is of immeasurable benefit and should be a priority when considering the inclusion of the child in nurseries, schools, clubs etc. Indeed, if they only have the opportunity to mix with other children who display atypical or undesirable behaviours, this could result in them imitating and learning inappropriate behaviour themselves.

It is too easy to focus on the 'special' needs of a child with a known condition and to forget their ordinary needs as children. In the case of children with fragile X, both their special and their ordinary needs are best served by inclusion in a mainstream setting for at least part of the time, and especially at an early age. By mixing with their peers they can also learn how to socialise and to develop skills that facilitate the making of friends who can provide good role models both in the short and hopefully the long term.

Assessment and testing

In an educational setting, one of the first tasks of the teacher is to find out what the child can do in order to establish the level at which he is currently functioning. Once an initial baseline has been established, the teacher can go on to plan a programme of work that is appropriate to the individual child.

The purpose of testing should not just be to ascertain a child's current level of functioning but also to discover his strengths and weaknesses and the areas in which he is particularly interested and which are motivating for him. It should also aim to discover the ways that the child likes to learn and the conditions under which he performs best. Assessment should therefore provide a starting point for the development of an individual programme that is appropriate to the child's needs. As that programme is carried out the teacher continues to assess performance and progress so that a more in-depth picture of the child is being developed all the time which in turn goes on to inform further teaching.

Teacher assessment

This is by far the most important and useful method of assessment as it enables one person to get to know the child over an extended period, to learn how he is likely to respond in a given situation, and how to get the best out of him. Information gleaned by observation over a longer period and in a number of situations both formal and informal are far more likely to yield reliable, useful information about the child's performance and abilities in all areas. Although it is time consuming and it may take a long time to gain an overall profile of the child, the time spent getting to know him and how he approaches his learning is invaluable. It is only when a teacher has a full assessment of the child's functioning and an understanding of how he learns, that she can plan an appropriate individual learning programme for him and teach it in a way that is most likely to be successful.

Formal assessment

There may be times in the life of a child with special needs when a formal assessment is needed, perhaps as a requirement in order to make a formal diagnosis of need, to allocate extra resources or to make a judgment about an appropriate placement. These more formal testing situations are often crucial to the future of a child, but unfortunately for the child with fragile X, and probably many others as well, the nature of the testing situation is likely to be problematic and he is unlikely to be able to perform to the best of his ability.

Many teachers report that their pupils with fragile X perform better on tasks in a regular classroom setting than they would expect from their score on an IQ test, which would suggest that the IQ test failed to measure the child's ability accurately or do justice to his skills. This might be because the tasks demanded of the child in an IQ test require more abstract thought than the tasks which are set in the classroom, and children with fragile X find abstract thinking considerably more difficult than practical tasks and those which are set within a more concrete context. However, it is also likely that the child did not do himself justice in a formal testing situation, especially if it was conducted in a single sitting by an unfamiliar adult, as is often the case.

The following guidelines provide advice on testing that will enable a tester to reach conclusions that best reflect the true ability of the child. They are useful in any test or work situation as they are based on good teaching practice for children with fragile X, which will also be applicable to other children and other situations.

Familiarity

It is unlikely that any child will perform well for an unfamiliar adult. The tester should therefore try to spend some time getting to know the child prior to the beginning of the test. It may also be helpful for the child to be accompanied at the test by a trusted person, who, even if they take no part in the assessment, might provide a reassuring and calming presence.

Similarly, the child should be familiar with the room in which the tests will be carried out, to avoid the chance of him being over-stimulated by all the new and different aspects of the room.

Timing

Most children perform best in the morning and children with fragile X are no different. However, the child should have had the opportunity to establish himself in school and to become settled in his familiar routines before being taken off for testing. It is likely to help the child if he is given prior warning of the different activity and if he can see how it is going to slot into the whole plan of his day. He can then feel reassured that normality will be resumed at a particular time.

It is also important to consider the effect of any medication that the child may be taking and to schedule the test for the time when he is likely to be most alert and able to concentrate, and least likely to be drowsy. It may be possible to manipulate the drug times on the particular day to give the child the best chance of success.

Calming

Ensure that the tester is familiar with the characteristics of children with fragile X, particularly their tendency to become over-stimulated and anxious in new or different situations and how that is likely to affect their performance. At present, as diagnoses of fragile X are still relatively uncommon, it should not be assumed that testers are familiar with the very specific needs of these children, even though they may have had many years' experience with children with special educational needs. Even if they are experienced with children with fragile X, they will still need to be told the ways to calm this specific child and the techniques that the teacher finds most useful to keep him focused and to refocus him should his attention wander. The tester is most likely to be very grateful for this specific information that will enable him or her to get the most out of the child. It might be possible for the teacher or learning support assistant to be present or to observe the testing situation and make comments on how typically the child is behaving or how better results might be achieved.

Duration

The child with fragile X is likely to perform better in short sessions, possibly even spread over several days if the schedule of the tester allows this. As concentration is often poor, long sessions with lots of different activities are likely to be hard for him.

By spreading the tests over several days, the child will become more familiar with the tester and the testing situation and the tester will be able to see differences in performance from one day to the next. These are often particularly great with children with fragile X. If the test is spread, these variations are more likely to even out and results be more valid. It may also be the case that a child who is oppositional and refuses to cooperate with the tester on one day, may be far more cooperative on another occasion.

Whatever the duration of the session, it is helpful for the child to be able to see what he has to complete before the session is over. A concrete or visual symbol of each activity that is going to be undertaken could be displayed and as each test is performed, the child could put the equipment or the picture away so that he can see, by the diminishing pile, exactly how many more tasks have to be completed. This will help him to retain concentration on the tasks and to know that the activities have a definite time-span, after which he can go. The tester should also be aware of how long the child can be expected to sit in one place and concentrate before needing a break. It is important that unrealistic expectations are not held here, as they are likely to cause distress and raise anxiety, resulting in reduced performance.

Relating to the child

The tester should be aware of the difficulties that the child may have in relation to social anxiety, for example their aversion to making eye-contact, answering questions directly etc. The tester should keep efforts at social contact low-key and non-threatening. He or she should not demand that the child makes eye-contact or shakes hands, and the type of preliminary 'chat' that might help to put another child at ease, such as asking about his hobbies or family, should be abandoned if the child is clearly not enjoying or responding to it.

The tester should position him or herself alongside or behind the child to introduce and administer the tests and avoid touching the child or looking directly into his eyes.

Direct questions

One of the most frustrating aspects of testing a child with fragile X is the knowledge that he may not provide the correct answer in a test when you know that he is able to do it in a different situation or if asked in a different way. This is characteristic of many children with learning difficulties but it is particularly true for children with fragile X and another reason why this type of formal testing should be kept to an absolute minimum. While a tester who is a stranger to the child has no way of knowing whether the child is performing to his true ability or knowledge, it is worth him or her being aware of this tendency and trying to rephrase questions or allow the child to demonstrate knowledge in a different way, if the child is not performing well.

Teaching strategies

There is an extent to which teaching children with fragile X is no different from teaching any child with special educational needs, or indeed from teaching any child at all. All children learn best in a situation where they feel secure, confident and approved of, where expectations are realistically high and where tasks set are challenging yet achievable. They all need a planned and structured programme that enables them to build on current skills to learn new ones, and to extend their knowledge in a systematic way. They respond to praise and the motivation of their own success.

There is a huge range of special educational needs that teachers must respond to, both in mainstream and special schools, and a huge range of strategies at their disposal to try to meet these needs. However, most children who are experiencing difficulties respond when offered a higher degree of individual attention, a more carefully structured programme with greater opportunity for repetition and/or reinforcement, an opportunity to have their specific difficulties addressed and when extra attention is given to motivation and developing the child's confidence in their own abilities.

With this understanding, and a great deal more knowledge and expertise that teachers have acquired as a result of their years of teaching, much of which has probably become second nature, it is possible for any good teacher to teach a child with fragile X quite successfully. Indeed, there are certainly many children with fragile X in our schools now who have not been diagnosed yet are making good progress. Teachers are skilled at responding to individual needs as they are presented, and a great deal of excellent teaching is the result of a teacher's intuitive responses to the needs of a child that she has come to know well.

However, children with fragile X do have a specific cognitive profile (described in Chapter 2), as well as individual cognitive characteristics, and they do have specific needs that arise as a result of their condition. It has also been proved through research and found through the experience of teachers and therapists, that there are specific ways of teaching and specific strategies that teachers can employ that are particularly effective with children with fragile X, and which enable them to function and learn more effectively. By understanding these, a teacher can become even more effective at meeting the needs of the child with fragile X, and can avoid unwittingly teaching in ways that may make life and learning more difficult for them.

At this point it may be useful to go back to Chapter 2 to refresh the memory about the cognitive characteristics associated with fragile X syndrome before going on to consider strategies that the teacher can employ to facilitate learning.

Teaching strategies – preparation and presentation

Preparing the child for work

Chapter 3 describes how the teacher can organise the classroom and the school day, and how she can make specific allowances that will make it easier for the child with fragile X to function effectively in the classroom. There is also much that can be done to prepare him for specific work sessions so that the child is at his most receptive and the sessions are as productive as possible. For many pupils with fragile X, it will not be necessary to make any special preparations for work sessions other than those that other children may require, but for some, time spent in preparation can be worthwhile so that the child is ready to learn and receptive to the teaching.

The work environment should be familiar to the child and should be a place that he associates with work rather than other activities. It should be as free from distractions as possible, and with furniture that he finds comfortable, so that he can forget about his surroundings and focus on the task in hand. For many children with fragile X the learning area is a desk in a quiet place in the classroom, preferably out of the way of the main activities and movement of the rest of the children and away from the door. Other people coming and going or moving around are likely to be hugely distracting for him and even the fact that the door *might* open and someone *might* come in, can be sufficiently distracting to make it hard for him to concentrate. Some teachers find it helpful to use mobile screens to block out the rest of the room and the activity of helping to put the screens in place can help the child to prepare himself for work.

It is worth trying to plan the child's individual sessions for the same time each day so that it can become part of his familiar and accepted routine. If this is not possible, it is helpful to tell the child at the beginning of the day when his individual session is going to be, perhaps by incorporating it into his daily schedule board, (see Chapter 3). The child can also be helped to make the transition from another activity to the work session by a reminder a few minutes before, that a change is coming or by telling him that he will be changing activity when he has completed a specified task.

If the child is clearly not settled and ready to learn, which may be evidenced by excessive hand-flapping, inability to sit still, preoccupation with other objects or activities, a refusal to cooperate etc., one of the following activities may help to calm and focus him:

- listening to a piece of calming music;
- talking about one of his favourite topics;
- reading a familiar story;
- deep breathing exercises;
- massaging a chosen area on the child's body;
- stroking slowly down the child's back, the next hand starting as the previous one reaches the bottom, so that continuous pressure is felt;
- playing with a familiar/favourite puzzle or game.

These are all fairly easy to do in most classrooms and do not require any special equipment or space. Over time the teacher will learn which of these or other strategies each child responds to best and these can be used when needed or incorporated into the daily routine.

Presentation of work

The way that work is presented to children with fragile X can make a great deal of difference to how successfully they are able to respond to it and complete it. Once the teacher is aware of this she can ensure that work is presented in a way that is likely to elicit the best response.

- Children with fragile X need to be very clear about what they are being asked to do and what is expected of them. As many have attention difficulties, tasks should be kept short and short-cuts allowed to enable them to get the satisfaction of completing a task within the limits of their concentration. For example, do not expect them to write full sentences for answers if single words will do.

- They will respond best when given clearly defined tasks where the requirements are explicit. They will also find it easier to complete tasks that have an unambiguous ending. For example, avoid tasks such as: 'See how many words you can write down beginning with t,' or 'See how many of the sums on page 34 you can do this lesson.' Replace such tasks with: 'Write down 10 words beginning with t,' or 'Do six sums from page 34.' When the child has an open-ended task, he is likely to lose concentration quickly. However if he can aim for a particular number, he is more likely to succeed. He will be further helped if he has ten specially drawn boxes on the page in which to put the ten words beginning with 't', or six spaces in which to do the six sums. This will help to focus him even more on the requirements of the task and keep him going to the end.

- Verbal instructions should be clear, and as simple and short as possible. The child is likely to be distracted by verbal 'clutter' in the instruction, so this should be avoided. For example: 'Put your coat on and go out to the playground' rather than 'I think it's about time for everyone to make their way out to play now, so off you go and don't forget coats, it's quite cold today.'

- Many children with fragile X will find it hard to follow more than one verbal instruction at a time so it is likely to be most effective to issue one instruction and wait for that to be completed before issuing the next. It may well be an important progression for the child to learn to respond to more than one instruction at a time, but it should be remembered that this may be quite difficult. To help, the teacher can issue the two instructions clearly and as concisely as possible, repeating them a number of times and getting the child to repeat back to her, what he has to do. It will help if a visual reminder is shown so that the child can internalise a picture of the task, and if the instruction has two parts, two pictures or symbols could be used. For example, if the instruction is to get a book and go to their desk to read it, a photograph of a book and then a photograph of a person reading at a desk could be put up in sequence, on a board that the child can see all the time. While photographs might be used initially, the progression should be to representational pictures, then symbols and finally words. With these visual prompts, the child is more likely to be able to accomplish the two-phased instruction. He could then progress to three or more parts to an instruction.

- If work is presented in written form, e.g. a worksheet, it should be kept simple and uncluttered, with just one task or question to each page. Written work is hard for them and the task of writing an answer to show that they know something is often so difficult that they fail with the writing and thereby fail to show that they know the fact. If they can circle or underline the right answer, or put a counter on the right one, they are more likely to succeed. Use of the computer can often enable them to demonstrate their knowledge quickly and effectively without the need to engage in the task of writing, which is fraught with difficulty for them.

Teaching strategies – teaching and learning

One of the skills possessed by a good teacher is the ability to adapt the way in which she teaches according to the learning needs of the individual pupil. While there may be similarities in the way different children learn, all children have their own preferred ways of learning and will be able to respond more quickly and easily to one approach rather than another. Good teachers are aware of the different ways that children can learn and aim to incorporate as much variety as possible in their teaching, to ensure that they accommodate the preferred learning styles of their pupils.

The majority of pupils are quite flexible and are capable of learning in a variety of ways; although they have a preferred learning style, they are still capable of learning and progressing even if their teacher does not always teach in the way they learn best. However, a child with special educational needs may find it more difficult to be flexible and may need to be taught in ways that suit his preferred style of learning and which take careful account of his cognitive strengths and weaknesses before he is able to learn effectively. For this reason it is particularly important for teachers of pupils with special educational needs to find out, through careful observation, assessment and experimentation, just how each pupil learns and which teaching techniques and strategies are most successful.

Children very enormously in their approaches to learning. This is certainly true of children with fragile X but their specific cognitive strengths and weaknesses predispose them to learn best in particular ways and they will respond best when the teacher takes this into account. This is not to say that they will all learn in exactly the same way as they will have individual traits as well as those brought about by their condition. However, with an understanding of the learning characteristics shared by many children with fragile X, the teacher has a useful starting point. She can go on to ascertain the extent to which her pupil displays the traits that are typical of the condition, and she can make informed decisions as to which teaching strategies are likely to be successful.

We will go on in this section to consider the specific cognitive strengths and weaknesses of children with fragile X, and consider the teaching strategies that have been found useful, and some which are definitely not to be recommended with these children.

Teaching strategies – building on cognitive strengths

Simultaneous processing v. sequential processing

Using the Kaufman Assessment Battery for Children (KABC), which is an assessment used extensively in research as it has been found to be useful in identifying the great variability in abilities often found in children with specific syndromes, Kemper *et al.* (1988) found that boys with fragile X perform better at tasks involving simultaneous processing than those involving sequential processing.

This needs some explanation.

Simultaneous processing is a function that requires the integration of stimuli to form a whole entity. Once a whole concept or idea or task has been understood or learned, providing the same stimuli or clues remain, the child can understand and respond correctly on future occasions, as required. However, if some components of the original idea are missing the child may have difficulty understanding or even recognising it again. The child learns and understands 'whole' entities, rather than seeing the component parts of them. He understands, almost intuitively, a whole process or picture, but has difficulty putting together individual parts to create a whole. This is one reason why the child with fragile X may not respond when asked a question, even though you know that he knows the answer. However, if you rephrase the question and try to use the terminology or ideas that were used when he first learnt the information, he is likely to be able to respond quite fully and well, showing a good understanding. It is likely that he did not recognise what you were asking on the first attempt, but the familiar words or ideas fitted with his understanding of the whole concept and unlocked it from his mind, giving him access to it and enabling him to show his knowledge.

Sequential processing on the other hand, involves putting ideas or component parts together in the correct sequence, in order to build up a skill or idea. For example: learning the steps to take to complete a task such as making a cake; putting phonic sounds together to spell a word; putting pictures in order to tell a story or following a set of instructions. Sequencing is something that boys with fragile X find very difficult.

This knowledge about the ability of boys with fragile X to learn better through simultaneous processing rather than sequential processing is of great importance to the classroom teacher, therapists, parents and anyone else who wishes to teach them something. However it is particularly important that the teacher understands this fact because it may well run counter to the general principles of good practice that she has used with children with special educational needs in the past. It is generally accepted that children with learning difficulties often need to have tasks broken up into smaller parts so that they are not overwhelmed by having to learn too great an amount at one time. By breaking the learning up into more manageable parts, they can learn an amount that is appropriate to their degree of ability, and eventually build up the skill by putting all the parts together. Teachers have been analysing tasks, breaking them down into smaller steps and gradually building them up by teaching one part at a time, for many years. It is often very helpful for children with learning difficulties to be taught in this way and for most teachers it is a well used teaching technique that they apply almost as a matter of course when a child is having difficulty learning something. However, from what we know about the learning styles of boys with fragile X, namely their difficulties with sequential processing and their relative strength at simultaneous processing, this teaching technique could well be making it hard for them to learn.

Our knowledge suggests that instead of breaking tasks down the teacher should endeavour to teach complete tasks. She should teach a complete task or present a whole process every time she teaches the child, repeating the process many times until the child has acquired the whole concept or learnt the skill. In this way the child can develop an understanding of the entire process. If he is taught only one small part of a skill, he will assume that the small part constitutes the whole skill and he will be able to repeat only that part. He may then learn other small parts successfully, leading the teacher to think that satisfactory progress is being made. But when he is expected to put the parts together to build up the whole, he will have tremendous difficulty and may never manage to perform the whole skill without prompting. However, if he is shown or taught the entire skill at every teaching session, he is more likely to master it, given time.

For example, when teaching the child to write his name (assuming that this is a skill that is appropriate to his current level of ability) the whole name, as he is likely to be asked to reproduce it, should be taught, e.g. David Brown. It is worth teaching the Christian name and surname together if it is likely that the child will eventually be able to write both, otherwise he will have to learn two separate tasks which he may always have difficulty performing at the same time, in the right order.

He should then practise the whole thing every time, rather than practising the individual letters in isolation. Even if initial attempts bear little relation to the name, persevere in shaping and improving the whole name rather than breaking it down and practising individual letters. You may expect him to write the first letter unaided and trace the others, moving on to writing the first two and tracing the others etc. etc. When learned in this way, the child will eventually know the correct way to write his name by having acquired the skill in its entirety. If he has learnt the letters individually he will always have difficulty putting them together in the right order and may never master it.

Teaching through the visual medium

Children with fragile X respond well to information that is presented visually and their learning is facilitated by the use of visual aids. Teachers find that using visual material to back up information or instructions that are delivered verbally makes a significant difference to whether it is remembered at a future date or responded to in the present.

For example:

- When teaching a skill such as making a sandwich or putting on a coat, it is helpful if the skill can be modelled a few times first by someone who does it well. In this way the child can see how it is done. They are good at imitating, and are generally interested in what people around them are doing, so learning by copying others is relatively easy and enjoyable for them.
- When teaching about animals, have the real live animal in the classroom, or a video, or a photograph. The child's memory will be greatly enhanced by being able to link the information to a mental picture of the information. He will also be aided in his ability to recall the information taught on that occasion by being shown the video or picture again, as the visual image has become linked in his mind with the information.
- When asking the child to do something, if he does not respond initially, he is often triggered to do so by a visual prompt alongside the verbal instruction. This might take the form of a picture of himself or another person doing the activity, e.g. putting on his coat, going into the lunch room and eating lunch etc. Once the child has become used to responding to one pictorial prompt, he may well be able to accomplish more complex tasks or instructions by following a series of visual instructions. A series of photographs or pictures or symbols could be pasted up in the correct order, for him to see and follow. In this way he might be able to carry out more difficult tasks than he would otherwise have been able to, e.g. turning on the computer and setting up a programme; getting the equipment out for PE; making a cup of tea etc.
- Visual prompts can be used to help the child to perform transitions that may be difficult for him as the visual image will help him to prepare himself for the coming activity.
- Signing to the child at the same time as talking can also be helpful, even if the child is able to understand normal speech. The additional visual prompt helps the child to focus and concentrate on the words, and provides additional, complementary sensory input to reinforce the words. Some children with fragile X find signs and/or symbols useful as a prelude to speech. It is common for children with fragile X to be late in speaking, and using some Makaton or similar manual signs to express needs or communicate desires before they are able to verbalise them can encourage them to appreciate the value and power of

communication and thereby motivate them to want to speak. Individualised symbol boards using photographs, pictures or established symbols such as Rebus or Blissymbolics can also have the same effect.

- Visual prompts can also be used to help the child to orientate himself in time through the day. A series of pictures of the activities that are going to happen, in order, can be very helpful in enabling the boy with fragile X to anticipate what is going to occur, and to see what else will be expected of him. Visual schedule boards are discussed in greater detail in Chapter 3.

Teaching through practical experiences

Kolb (1984) describes four different learning styles and suggests that everyone will tend towards one or more of these and find it easier to learn new things in these ways. The learning styles are:

- preference for concrete experience;
- preference for reflective observation;
- preference for abstract conceptualisations;
- preference for active experimentation.

The child with fragile X will tend towards a learning style that favours concrete experience and active experimentation. He finds it hard to sit at a desk for long and prefers to be able to move around as he engages in a practical task. He finds it difficult to process or manipulate ideas mentally, i.e. to reflect on information, form mental concepts and think in an abstract way, but he can engage in a practical task that involves the manipulation of concrete objects and can act almost intuitively to solve problems or arrive at solutions through active experimentation.

Teachers report that the activities favoured by children with fragile X are almost exclusively practical, with swimming, P.E., music and art or craft being the most popular (Saunders 1997). They also highlight the fact that the ability of the boys to carry out tasks involved in daily living and in the life of the classroom is far higher than the teacher would expect from a knowledge of their cognitive functioning.

The teacher can capitalise on the relative strength of boys with fragile X to learn through practical, concrete experiences in many ways.

For example:

- Using real objects and real situations to teach skills.

The child will learn how to prepare a simple dish such as beans on toast far more quickly if he has the opportunity to be helped through the process and make it for his lunch. He is less likely to learn to do it by discussing how it should be done, making a list of the steps to take or putting a series of photographs in the right order.

Similarly, he will learn about one-to-one correspondence better by giving out drinks and straws to all the pupils in the class rather than sitting at a desk drawing lines between objects in a work-book.

Finally, he will learn what animals need to live better by looking after the class gerbil for a week rather than listening to a teacher telling him and performing a writing or drawing task.

- Allowing the child to physically manipulate objects to find things out.

He will learn that round things roll faster than flat-sided ones by letting them travel down a ramp rather than hypothesising about what might happen.
He will find out that structures need a solid foundation to stand up by being allowed to build some that haven't and watching them fall down.
He will learn which things float and sink by putting them in water himself rather than watching the teacher do it.

- Using practical activities to bring the acquisition of information to life.

A unit on Ancient Egypt can include a project to build pyramids in different materials.
A unit on life underground can include time spent making tunnels in wet sand and spending some time in a play tunnel to see how it is easiest to move.
A unit on the Nineteenth Century can include spending a morning seeing how they can exist without using anything electrical.

Children with fragile X are far more likely to be able to recall information from topic work if they have experienced some enjoyable, practical activities of this nature rather than being given information in verbal form, however interesting the teacher has made it.

Of course, it is not only children with fragile X who benefit from and learn better through practical and concrete activities. Children in the early years, both chronologically and developmentally, learn in this way as they have not yet reached the developmental age at which they can replace physical activity with mental representation of the physical task. A large number of children with special educational needs also learn better in this way for the same reason. Consequently, many teachers of young or less academically able children will be very experienced at providing practical experiences through which their pupils can learn. However it is worth remembering that children with fragile X are not always simply developmentally young and learning in this way because it is appropriate to their cognitive developmental level. They do have a specific preference for acquiring new information in this particular way and once it has been acquired they may be able to demonstrate their understanding in a more advanced way.

Having stated that children with fragile X learn best in this practical way through concrete experiences, it must also be remembered that certain aspects of their condition also make practical activity hard at some levels. For example: their tactile defensiveness may make it unpleasant for them to handle some materials; their impulsivity may mean that they rush at tasks and don't spend sufficient time on them to complete them as well as they might or their lack of good fine motor skills may make it hard to manipulate small objects very effectively or cut, stick, fold etc. These are not reasons to avoid the activities as the child will still learn best in these ways, but the teacher should bear them in mind at the lesson planning stage so that ways can be found to make it easier for the child to succeed at the task.

Teaching through areas of high interest

While it is true that all people learn better when the content of the learning is of interest to them, this is particularly true of children with fragile X syndrome. Teachers often report that they are amazed at the amount and the complexity of the information that their pupil with fragile X can master when it is concerned with a topic of particular interest.

Many children with fragile X have specific interests which in some cases might be considered to be obsessions. Typical interests include cars, wheels, a fictional character such as Fireman Sam, football teams, etc. etc. Although these interests might appear to be counterproductive in some instances as the child can be so fixated by their interest that they find it hard to leave them and learn about or enjoy other things, they can also be very useful for the teacher to use to teach other things.

For example the child who is interested in cars may well learn to count cars, sort cars into colours or makes, read about cars, find out about the production process, learn about the countries that different cars come from, etc. etc. The opportunities are endless for the inventive teacher. One interest can also be expanded to encourage the child to broaden their interest or move on to something else. For example cars may lead on to an interest in aeroplanes and flight or travel.

Teaching through humour

Children with fragile X often have a well developed sense of humour and respond well to humour in the classroom. They often enjoy cartoons and jokes and slapstick situations and a tense or anxious situation that might lead to an outburst of temper can often be diffused by a joke. Their love of humour can be used in their learning in several ways, for example:

- The teacher can teach them to read the words in the speech bubbles of cartoon characters.
- They can write their own 'knock knock' jokes and share them with another child.

- They can keep a running list of favourite jokes to practise handwriting or computer use.
- They can role-play a humourous situation with another child to encourage interaction.

Teaching strategies – taking account of cognitive weaknesses

It is necessary for the class teacher to be aware of the areas of weakness in terms of cognitive functioning that children with fragile X experience, partly so that she can avoid trying to teach the child specifically using methods that the child will have difficulty responding to and partly so that she can take specific action to help to develop the child in the areas of weakness. While it may seem unhelpful to concentrate on areas of weakness, as part of a balanced programme that also gives plenty of opportunity to use and develop strengths, action to help the child to develop in the areas that he finds difficult will help him in his daily life, and enable him to learn more effectively.

Sequencing

Sequencing can be described as any task that requires the child to put items in a desired order. Anything that involves sequencing is hard for a child with fragile X. This means that a huge range of tasks are likely to cause difficulty. These include:

- writing words – which requires the sequencing of letters;
- reading unfamiliar words – which requires the breaking down of words;
- number work – which relies on an understanding of the sequence and size of numbers;
- everyday tasks which require the child to perform a series of steps in the right order;
- following instructions;
- following a timetable of events through the day or week;
- putting pictures in order of time, objects in order of size etc. etc.

These examples are sufficient to show that a weakness in sequencing is likely to cause difficulties in many, if not most, areas of school life and specific work to improve these skills will improve performance and make it easier for the child to learn.

Remedial help for sequencing will require the teacher to be aware of the child's current level of ability in this area and provide opportunities to practise the skill at an appropriate level and with the appropriate degree of support, to gradually improve his abilities. For example:

- if the child can follow a two part instruction, he can be helped to extend this to three;

- if he can spell a three letter phonically regular word, he can be taught to cope with words with more letters or sounds.

It is perhaps the teacher's awareness of the child's problem that is most important as she can be understanding of his difficulties, not expect too much of him too soon, and be aware that the skill will need to be developed gradually. She can also provide specific help in the classroom when tasks involving sequencing are required, so that the child is not left to fail with a task that is beyond his capabilities.

Specific strategies that may help the child to cope in the classroom despite having difficulty with sequencing include:

- providing a written or pictorial reminder of sequences that have to be followed. The child could be taught to cover up each step as he performs it so that he doesn't lose his place and can see clearly where he is in the sequence;
- teaching reading by whole-word rather than phonic methods, at least initially;
- teaching spelling by encouraging the child to memorise the look of the whole word rather than encouraging the breaking down of the word into separate sounds;
- providing him with a number line of the appropriate length that he can always refer to;
- always modelling a new task;
- teaching skills by many repetitions of the whole skill rather than building it up step by step;
- using the teaching strategies of shaping a response or gradually fading or reducing the amount of help given for the child to complete the task, rather than using a step by step approach.

Memory

It is generally accepted that children with fragile X have difficulties with tasks requiring memory. However, parents and teachers often report that they can be amazed at their child's ability to memorise information on a topic that is of particular interest to them and their ability to recall in detail an event that happened long ago that was of special significance to them. There is clearly some discrepancy here. Memory involves the receiving and holding of information, its organization into a form that is meaningful, its internalization and assimilation with existing information that is on the same or a similar topic, and the ability to recall and express the information when required.

The child with fragile X has difficulty with short-term memory, the ability to take in and hold new information, but once that information has passed into the long-term memory it is more likely to be remembered. As his difficulty with short-term memory is likely to cause him problems in his everyday life, exercises to develop short-term memory can be used, but the teacher can also help the child to cope by teaching him strategies to compensate. These may include:

- providing a book to carry with him that contains information that he may find hard to remember, e.g. address, phone number, clothes sizes etc.;
- teaching the child to repeat back new information to encourage him to focus on it;
- giving a visual picture to link new information with old in his mind.

He may also have difficulty recalling information when required. We know that children with fragile X have difficulty answering a direct question even when it is known that they know the answer. However the same child may well demonstrate his knowledge by telling another child or muttering it when another child is asked the same question. It would appear that the child becomes so anxious when he is put 'on the spot' that he is unable to recall the information required. It may also be that he is unable to find the words to express the idea that he has in his head. In a more relaxed session he may be able to chat freely about the same topic.

The implication here for the teacher is that the child with fragile X needs help to recall the information that he has stored.

Strategies to help include:

- avoiding asking direct questions to the child, especially when he is in a group or any setting that he finds stressful;
- being aware of what the child is saying or demonstrating when other children in the class or group are being asked a question;
- not assuming that he doesn't know something just because he cannot tell you on one occasion;
- trying to make the child as relaxed as possible before asking a question;
- asking the child to explain something to another child rather than an adult;
- having a 'chat' or playing a game to find out what he knows;
- showing a picture that might help him to recall something;
- allowing him to demonstrate knowledge in other ways than verbally;
- teaching whenever possible in a meaningful context so that the child can be reminded of the context to help him access the information, e.g. 'do you remember what we learned when we went for the nature walk and stopped under the huge oak tree?'

Motor planning and fine motor skills

Motor planning is the ability to plan the motor movements involved in any physical task that we are going to perform, e.g. laying a table, climbing steps, opening an envelope etc. Children with fragile X find it hard to prepare themselves to execute such tasks in a smooth, flowing way and this, coupled with their difficulties with tasks involving fine motor control, makes it hard for them to do many of the tasks required in a classroom.

The most prominent difficulty that they face, especially as they get older, is in handwriting. Handwriting involves tiny motor movements of the hand, applying the right amount of pressure both on the pencil and the paper, and then planning how to move the pencil in the correct way to form the letters. This requires enormous concentration and effort on the part of the child with fragile X and even when they are theoretically able to write, the effort involved means that they quickly get mentally and physically tired and they are unable to sustain the necessary degree of concentration for long. While writing is a necessary skill in everyday life and if possible, the child should be encouraged to develop and practise the skill so that he can fill in forms, sign his name, write lists and notes etc., the teacher should think very carefully how much writing it is appropriate to expect of the child with fragile X. There are many ways of reducing the amount of writing that the child has to do, for example:

- allow him to use a computer or lap-top word-processor. For many this provides an easy and effective solution;
- produce worksheets where the child can fill in single words, circle correct answers, tick an option etc.;
- allow him to talk into a tape recorder;
- allow him to draw a picture or diagram or make a chart;
- allow him to make answers verbally to an adult or more able peer.

Using these alternative means to display knowledge, writing can be saved for occasions when alternatives are not possible. The scenario to be avoided is when the child is compelled to write lengthy amounts in the erroneous belief that it will improve his writing and that it will get easier for him if he practises more. The reality is that it will probably get worse as he becomes exhausted, and he will fail to display the extent of his knowledge as the physical effort of the writing process is so great that he has no reserves left to think about the quality of what he is producing. It is important to practise writing skills, but the maxim of 'a little and often' is preferable. The teacher needs to be aware of the difficulties that he faces in writing and ensure that the demands placed upon him are realistic and not counter-productive.

Generalising

This can be defined as the ability to transfer knowledge learned in one situation to another different but appropriate situation. It requires the child to understand the essential purpose of the learning and its component parts, to recognise another situation which they deem sufficiently similar to warrant the same behaviour, and to reproduce the original behaviour under similar but not identical circumstances. Children with fragile X, in common with many other children with learning difficulties, find it very difficult to do this. Behaviour or skills that have been learnt in one setting can often only be reproduced in the identical setting. Similarly, knowledge that has been acquired in the classroom can often not be demonstrated outside it, e.g. the child may be able to handle simple purchases and money transactions in a classroom but unable to function in a shop.

It is necessary to make general a specific part of the teaching of any skill or piece of knowledge. Once the child has mastered a skill in one way, this should be followed up by strategies that enable him to practise it in different situations. It should not be considered that the skill is mastered until it can be demonstrated in a number of different settings. For example: If the child can add two numbers in a one-to-one situation with the class teacher, he could be encouraged to generalise the skill by:

- adding numbers:
  with a different member of staff;
  with other children in a group;
  in a different place;
  using different counters or concrete aids;
  in practical situations around the class;
- using the skill in situations around the school;
- using the skill at home;
- adding the greatest number first or second;
- adding a third number to the first total etc.

Self-organisation

The skill of self-organization requires the child to remember the things that he has to do, recall them when necessary, and carry them out in the right order or sequence.

As we have already stated, all these cause difficulties for children with fragile X. Consequently, many of them find it very difficult to carry out the simplest of tasks in the classroom without either frequent reminders about what to do next, or a person to assist in the organization of the child and the task. Many teachers report that the child with fragile X is very demanding in terms of adult time as he often needs one-to-one attention before he can accomplish the things that are required of him. It is often not that the tasks themselves are too hard, but the organisation required to approach and accomplish them are beyond him.

Ironically, once the child has managed to learn a useful routine that enables him to organise himself to carry out an activity, he is likely to become very rigid about it and have great difficulty in changing it or having change imposed on him. This may well be because, having struggled to learn a routine that enables him to function successfully he is naturally reluctant to give it up.

We have already described how sequences of visual prompts that he can follow can help the child to work through a task. Once the child has learnt the skill of following the visual prompts, it can be possible to change their content without causing too much distress to the child.

Other strategies that can help the child to organise himself include:

- offering adult help that gradually fades out as the child takes on more of the organisation;
- pairing the child with a more able child who can act as a role model.

Slow processing time

Children with fragile X often find it difficult to think or react quickly when asked a question or asked to do something. They need to be given time to produce a considered answer. The word 'considered' is crucial here as they are often very impulsive in their responses and will rush in with an answer or rush to engage in a task without having given it the necessary thought. Consequently, their answer is often wrong or they begin a task without a clear idea of how to proceed. Teachers often report that they rush their work and consequently make a poor job of it, when with help to slow down they do it far better. Therefore the teacher should encourage the child to stop and think before responding to a question or a request, but should then be prepared for a longer than usual wait, during which time she should remain silent to give him a chance to process the question and formulate a response. Any interruptions are likely to distract the child and break his train of thought.

Conclusion

Different teaching strategies are always required to suit the learning needs of different pupils. In this chapter we have looked at specific learning strengths and weaknesses that are commonly associated with children with fragile X syndrome, and have identified strategies that the teacher can use to take account of these characteristics and give children with fragile X the best possible chance of succeeding. Some of the strategies described will also suit other pupils with learning difficulties and may be practised with other children. It is likely that many will respond well to an approach that favours highly visual teaching and opportunities for active experimentation and concrete experiences. Other strategies such as teaching whole tasks or skills rather than dividing them up into smaller parts may be more specific to pupils with fragile X.

If the teacher is able to incorporate some or all of these strategies into her teaching it is likely that her pupils with fragile X will progress faster and find learning easier and consequently more rewarding. Enjoyment and the confidence brought about by success are crucial factors in all types of learning, and success in school can lead to other gains and have a positive effect on many other aspects of a child's life.

CHAPTER 5

Social and Behavioural Development

Behaviour in the classroom

This chapter concentrates on the types of behaviour commonly displayed by children with fragile X in classroom settings. These children often display behaviour that is unhelpful to themselves and disruptive to the routines and smooth running of the classroom and teachers and parents often agree that management of the child's behaviour is a priority when planning an individual programme. Clearly, these behaviours will not be confined to the classroom and many of them will occur in many or all areas of the child's life. Therefore, much of the advice offered to teachers about behaviour in classroom settings will be equally applicable to parents, friends, therapists and others who are concerned to help these young people to behave in ways that are most helpful to themselves and those around them.

In research by Saunders (1997) special school teachers were questioned about the behaviour exhibited by their pupils with fragile X in different circumstances throughout the school day.

When asked which, if any aspects of the child's behaviour they found difficult within the classroom, teachers reported:

- their extreme reactions to change or things that they did not like;
- their tendency to be noisy and therefore distracting to others;
- their propensity to physical aggression towards others;
- their inability to stay in their desk;
- their distractibility;
- their need for one-to-one adult attention in order to work.

The things that were cited as likely to trigger these undesirable behaviours were:

- unusual occurrences in the class;
- changes in the child's routine that he found intolerable;
- sudden noises;
- the bad behaviour of other pupils;
- not wishing to comply with the requests of the teacher.

It was found that in situations that they enjoyed and where they were happy to participate in the activity, they were likely to become excited and more physically active than usual, moving around more, laughing, talking, jumping and perhaps hand-flapping as well. It would appear, as might be expected, that enjoyment of a task also helped them to concentrate and perform better. As the majority of the most enjoyed activities were practical, with an emphasis on the physical, this increased activity was not felt to be problematic.

The situations that they did not enjoy and which they found most difficult were overwhelmingly often those involving large gatherings e.g. dinner-time, Assembly, playtime or whole-class sessions, especially if there was a high degree of noise and seemingly disorganised bustle. In these situations they became more physically active again and also more vocal. However, in these instances they were clearly distressed and some would run around the room as if in a panic, perhaps also hand-flapping and biting, kicking furniture, objects and sometimes people and making loud noises or repeating words or phrases over and over again. Some would also try to leave the room or 'escape' by hiding their head. The impression given is that the child has become over-aroused by the excessive amount of stimuli that he is experiencing and is in danger of losing control if he has not actually done so. He is trying to escape from or block out the source of his anxiety or confusion, or to regain some degree of security or control by resorting to his own safe, familiar, ritualistic activities.

All of these findings are consistent with other research and literature. The Fragile X Society, in their introductory guide to the education needs of children with fragile X, list the behaviours that can be expected of a child with fragile X as:

- overactivity or hyperactivity
- impulsivity
- inattention
- social anxiety
- mimicry
- liking for routines
- repetitive behaviours.

They go on to explain that children with fragile X are not exactly 'badly behaved' in the generally accepted sense, which implies some degree of intention, but their behaviours may well present teachers with management problems in the classroom.

However, just because a child may have a predisposition to a range of behaviours as a result of having a specific syndrome such as fragile X, it does not mean that he is obliged to exhibit those behaviours all his life, or that the undesirable behaviours have to be tolerated or excused by those around them. As Gibb (1996) points out, children with fragile X vary a great deal in the number of 'typical' traits that they display and also in the degree to which they display them. Like any child, they are also going to be affected by their past experiences and the environment in which they have grown up. Their behaviour will be partly governed by their condition, partly by their own personality, and partly by what they have learnt through their past experiences. If they have found that having a tantrum gets them what they want, they are more likely to have another tantrum next time they don't get their own way. If, however, they learn that their tantrum has no effect on the outcome, it is less likely to be repeated.

Fragile X and autism

It has long been recognised that many children with fragile X display some of the same behaviours as children on the autistic continuum. Indeed, many children with fragile X are initially wrongly diagnosed as having autism (and may continue to be wrongly diagnosed). Behaviours such as gaze-avoidance, social anxiety, repetitive behaviours such as hand-flapping or hand-biting, ritualistic behaviour, obsessive behaviour etc., may be common to both conditions. In research by Saunders (1997) 63 per cent of teachers felt that their pupils with fragile X displayed symptoms of autism.

As the two groups of children share a significant number of characteristics, the link between them has been the subject of much debate and research over the past two decades. In 1985, researchers such as Gillberg and Wahlstrom suggested that up to 25 per cent of autistic people may have fragile X syndrome. Fisch (1989) suggests that fragile X may actually be a causal factor for autism. Brown *et al.* (1986) suggest that fragile X is the single most common cause of autism and recommend that all people diagnosed with autism should be tested for fragile X.

However, more recent research has questioned the strong link between the two conditions that was found in these early studies. Payton *et al.* (1989) found a 2.4 per cent incidence of fragile X in the autistic sample that they studied, and suggest that this is no greater than that found generally in males with mental retardation. Piver *et al.* (1991) found that 2.7 per cent of autistic males in their study tested positive for fragile X and concluded that it was unlikely to be a causal factor in the autism. Bailey *et al.* (1993), in a large study, found only a 1.6 per cent link.

Turk (1997) sheds more important light on the subject as he discusses the fact that while the two groups of people share some common features, there are important features that distinguish them. People with autism have an indifference to social interaction and do not appear to want it when it is offered or seek it out. People with fragile X, however, are often highly desirous of human contact and are friendly, outgoing individuals. They do display anxiety in social situations, particularly with new people and in unfamiliar circumstances and this is likely to manifest itself in gaze-avoidance, but even when avoiding the gaze of the other person, the rest of their body language may be giving a different message and they often adopt an 'approach and retreat' pattern of behaviour that appears to indicate that they want to pursue the interaction but have difficulty doing so. Indeed, teachers and parents report that their children with fragile X are highly social and love the company of familiar and trusted adults and children.

In conclusion, it remains unclear whether there is a link between autism and fragile X, but if there is, it is unlikely to be as strong as was once thought. Clearly, it is possible for an individual to have both conditions together, but there may be no stronger link than that. While many of the characteristics of the conditions are similar, careful observation of the behaviours of the two groups suggest that they may not be as similar as appears at first glance and the reasons for the similar behaviours may be quite different. Therefore, when thinking about interventions to help people with fragile X, it is not helpful to make too much of the similarities with autism, nor to assume that what will help one group will automatically be useful for the other.

Fragile X and Attention Deficit Hyperactivity Disorder (ADHD)

Miezejeski and Hinton (1992) state that Attention Deficit Disorders (ADD), with or without hyperactivity, are the most commonly reported behavioural difficulties associated with fragile X. Freund (1994), states that the research literature is consistent in reporting significant problems with attention, hyperactivity and impulsiveness in children with fragile X and quotes past research that suggests that the percentage of males with hyperactivity lies within a range extending from 65 per cent to 93 per cent. Mazzocco and O'Connor (1993) suggest that males with fragile X show evidence within the brain of frontal lobe dysfunction which lends support to the theory that they suffer from damage to the parts of the brain involved in managing attentional processes.

Freund (1994) also states that research suggests that the hyperactive behaviour usually begins at about two years of age and is most marked during the years of primary schooling, decreasing with the onset of puberty. Turk (1997) reports that whereas some studies have refuted the fact that children with fragile X are any more likely to have ADD or ADHD than any other child with similar levels of learning difficulty, current thinking is that they are indeed more likely to show evidence of inattentiveness, restlessness and fidgetiness than other boys of the same age and ability.

As a link with ADD and ADHD appears to be more conclusive than that with autism, and it is quite clear that many children with fragile X do suffer attention difficulties, and/or hyperactivity and/or impulsivity, it is worth looking at the literature on ADHD and in particular at the strategies suggested for intervention, to assess how much may be relevant and useful for teaching children with fragile X. Cooper and Ideus (1996) list the behaviour that marks the child with ADHD as including all or some of the following:

- being out of seat too frequently;
- deviating from what the rest of the class is supposed to be doing;
- not following the teacher's instructions or orders;
- talking out of turn or calling out;
- being aggressive towards classmates;
- having a short attention span and being distractible;
- bothering classmates by talking or intruding on their work efforts;
- being oblivious or day-dreaming;
- losing and forgetting equipment;
- handing homework in late or not at all;
- handing in incomplete or sloppy work.

Many of these can also be applied to children with fragile X. Some of the strategies used to help children improve their concentration will be discussed later.

Understanding the behaviour

The behaviours that children exhibit based on their neurology influence their cognitive characteristics. The ways in which children cognitively understand the world around them in turn influence their behaviour.

(Schopmeyer and Lowe 1992, p. 34)

This encapsulates the important fact that cognitive function and behaviour are inextricably linked. One will always affect the other and development in one area will lead to subsequent improvement in the other.

Some of the behaviour of children with fragile X can be attributed to factors within the child. These have been explained and discussed in detail in Chapter 2. To sum up:

Movement
Low muscle tone and connective tissue disorder, tactile defensiveness and poorly developed vestibular and proprioceptive systems can all make gross and fine motor tasks extremely difficult so that they require enormous effort and concentration.

Understanding and responding to the environment
This is a function that relies on the ability to receive and make sense of environmental stimuli through the senses. The boys' hyper-sensitivity to sensory

stimuli, their limited ability to select important stimuli and ignore others and their poor sensory integration skills mean that they may not experience the world in the same way that other people do and they inhabit a world which is often overwhelming, confusing and hard to control.

Communication

Their difficulties with language delay, articulation and speech production, as well as their social anxiety, make it hard for them to enjoy normal social contact and to make friends, to find out about the world by asking questions and conversing with others, and to make clear to others the difficulties that they experience.

Academic performance

Their specific learning deficits make academic work difficult, especially if it is taught and they are expected to learn using skills that they do not possess.

In total, we can see that life in general and particularly life in the classroom where much is expected of each child and many skills are required, can be very challenging for the child with fragile X for reasons that an unenlightened teacher may not even be able to guess at. It is hardly surprising that a child who is overwhelmed by the bombardment of stimuli that he is receiving finds it hard to concentrate on the story that the teacher is reading, or a child who feels posturally insecure and cannot control his body sufficiently well to perform fine motor tasks has trouble eating without getting in a mess, or a child who is anxious or scared about activities that occur in a large group is reluctant to go into the hall for Assembly. A child with fragile X may be experiencing all these difficulties almost permanently, and many more.

If coping with the routines of daily living is so challenging and requires such immense effort and concentration it is hardly surprising that on occasion, or when one more pressure is added, the child cannot take any more and loses control. Perhaps what is more surprising is that it doesn't occur more often. What these children need is people around them who understand the difficulties that they experience and the effort that they are making to cope. Teachers need to know the precise nature of the difficulties that the child experiences so they can make life easier for them in some ways while making realistic and appropriate demands on them to develop their coping skills. They need to be aware of the likely effect of changes and challenges on the child with fragile X and to introduce them in such a way, with the necessary support, to enable them to meet them confidently.

I am not suggesting that bad behaviour should be permitted or ignored or that teachers should accept behaviour that is disruptive to others or unhelpful to the child in the long term. However, I do suggest that the teacher should be aware of the causes that may be contributing to the behaviour and what life is like for the child with fragile X in their class. It is only with this understanding that the teacher can go on to tackle the behaviour sensitively and effectively.

An approach to behaviour management

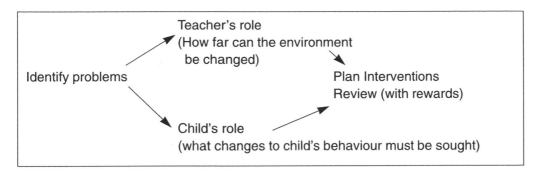

Figure 5.1

McNamara and Moreton (1995) state that behaviour is a combination of a response to the immediate stimuli in the classroom, coupled with a replication of previously learned behaviour.

Figure 5.1 shows a useful way of tackling behaviour that is causing a problem with children with fragile X. It acknowledges that problem behaviour is partly to do with the child and the way he reacts to events, but also partly to do with the environment that he is in and the expectations that are imposed on him.

Identify problems

Before embarking on any programme or intervention designed to effect change, it is essential to identify and clearly define the problems that need to be solved or, in this case, the specific behaviour that is causing problems and which needs to be changed. This should be done after careful and systematic observation of the child over some time and in different settings. It should also be done in consultation with parents if at all possible and with other relevant professionals.

Problems should be clearly defined
It is likely that different people perceive a problem in a slightly different way, according to their own perspective on it, e.g. a child may be rushing the work tasks set for him – the teacher may find this a problem because he never produces work that reflects his ability, while the assistant may be more concerned that when he has rushed the task, he wanders round the room and upsets other children. Therefore it is crucial that everyone involved has a very clear idea of the actual problem that is to be addressed. It may be more appropriate to define the problem not in terms of behaviour that is to be reduced, but in terms of the required behaviour that is to be increased. For example, 'the child will not rush his work' is better defined as, 'the

child will increase time spent on written tasks set'. It is then possible to go on to set clear objectives to facilitate change.

Problems should be prioritised
To do this, decisions must be made regarding:

Which behaviours are most detrimental to the child's current development in terms of physical, learning, and/or social and emotional needs?
Which are most detrimental to his long-term development?
Which are most disruptive to his family and impinge on the lives of family members?
Is this an appropriate time in the child's and other adults lives to tackle this?

Behaviour diary

One way of beginning to identify which aspects of a child's behaviour are particularly problematic, perhaps because of their frequency, their intensity, their effect on others or their cumulative effect on the child, is to keep a behaviour diary. This should be maintained over a sufficiently long period, e.g. one month, so that it is possible to get a picture that reflects normality, rather than an atypical picture which has resulted from an isolated change or upset. At this early stage, the purpose of the diary is simply to see objectively what is happening in terms of behaviour. This may not always be what staff think is happening as it is very easy to get a distorted view of the reality when subjectively involved.

As it is an attempt to find out what is normally happening in terms of behaviour, staff should not do anything specific to try to change behaviour during the time the diary is being kept, apart from the things that they would normally do with all the children, e.g. expect rules to be obeyed, use praise and incentives to encourage desirable behaviour, apply sanctions if this is part of the normal proceedings etc. Within the normal environment of discipline, the teacher should note down behaviours which are considered unacceptable. At the end of the specified period, staff and parents can use the diary to check out their own perceptions of what behaviours are most unacceptable.

The ABC method of recording and analysing behaviour

Having decided exactly which behavioral problem should be addressed at the current time, it is necessary to find out as much about that behaviour as possible, e.g. when, where, why, how often, with whom etc. etc. does it occur. A useful method to use to begin to answer these questions is the ABC – Antecedents, Behaviour and Consequences – model of recording and analysing behaviour. More information about this is given by Westmacott and Cameron (1981). In brief, the teacher records what happened just before the targeted behaviour occurred, the behaviour itself, and what happened just afterwards as a consequence. As these records are built up it is often possible to see a pattern or trend that might explain why the behaviour is happening.

For example, if a child with fragile X is having frequent tantrums it may be possible to see that they always occur when the child is coming up to a change of activity or when other children in the class are arguing. Or it may be that after a tantrum, the child is always taken to a quiet place and given the exclusive attention of a learning support assistant. He may find this so pleasurable that the consequence is actually causing the behaviour to be repeated. Having discovered the reasons for the behaviour or having made a hypothesis about possible causes, the teacher is in a more informed position to begin a programme of change.

In conclusion, having identified the behaviours that are causing difficulties for the child and those around him, and analysed them as far as possible, it is possible to plan systematically to reduce or eliminate them and to increase other more acceptable and helpful ones.

The teacher's role in effecting behavioural change

Before deciding on interventions to change the child's behaviour, it is important that the teacher considers how far she can eliminate or alleviate the problem by making changes within the classroom or adapting her expectations. In the case of children with fragile X it is possible for the teacher to organise the classroom, structure the day and set expectations at a point where the child is able to cope and finds it easier to behave in a way that is acceptable. In this way, the teacher can be said to be managing the child's behaviour by managing the environment in which he operates. We have already discussed, in Chapter 3, how a teacher can create a classroom environment conducive to success for a child with fragile X.

The ideas below focus specifically on creating an environment that encourages acceptable behaviour.

Ways in which the teacher can help to reduce the child's undesirable behaviour in the classroom include:

- having a well-defined routine to the day which is adhered to with as few changes as possible;
- maintaining a calm, ordered and relatively quiet classroom atmosphere;
- allowing the child to develop and follow familiar routines;
- not expecting child to stay in his seat for long periods, but allowing him to move around the room periodically;
- being aware of situations that he finds particularly hard to cope with and providing support;

- preparing the child for transitions;
- being realistic about expectations for work and behaviour;
- making expectations very clear to child;
- keeping work sessions short but focused;
- keeping distractions to a minimum;
- keeping change, unexpected events and upset to a minimum;
- providing a 'safe' personal space in the classroom for the child to retreat to when necessary;
- avoiding pressure to join in large group activities;
- avoiding asking direct questions or putting child under undue pressure.

If the teacher was able to comply with all these conditions it is likely that she would reduce the level of undesirable behaviour exhibited by the child in her class with fragile X. However, I would suggest that it is almost impossible to maintain these conditions 100 per cent of the time and indeed they may not be conducive to learning for some of the other children in the class. Neither is it helpful to the child to remove all need to learn strategies for coping in less than perfect situations. Clearly, it is vital that the child be helped to accept the world as it is with all its unexpected twists, its distractions and its pressures.

The task for the teacher therefore is to make a judgment about how far to manipulate the environment in order to make it easier for the child with fragile X and how far to expect him to cope by controlling or changing his own behaviour. The judgment will obviously be affected by the child's age, his developmental level, the specific difficulties that he experiences, the degree of control over his behaviour he already exercises, and the needs of the rest of the class. I would suggest that the greater his difficulties and the lower his age and developmental level, the more the teacher will need to manipulate the environment. As the child develops, more can be expected of him, more interventions for change can be implemented and more strategies taught for self control.

Interventions to change behaviour

The role of medication

The child with fragile X may require medication for a number of the physical or medical problems that he experiences, for example, to control epileptic seizures, to treat ear infections, to control gastro-oesophageal reflux etc. The use of medication to control some of his behaviour difficulties is more controversial. I am not going to suggest whether it is advisable or even helpful to use such medication as each case must be considered on its own merits by parents and the appropriate professionals who know the child and his history well. However, a description of the medications available and their possible effects will give readers some basic information on which to make the decision whether or not to pursue this type of intervention further.

It is sometimes possible to use drugs to help control the most distressing extremes of aggression, obsessive behaviour, and self-injury displayed by a minority of children with fragile X. These interventions are beyond the scope of this book. However, perhaps the main behaviour that is currently thought to be helped by medical intervention is that of attention-deficiency with or without hyperactivity, which is displayed to a significant degree by many children with fragile X syndrome.

The first and possibly most acceptable medical intervention, as it is a dietary component found commonly in many of the foods we eat, is folic acid. Turk (1992) summarises the research that has been done over the past decade to establish its efficacy after anecdotal evidence from parents and teachers regarding its usefulness in controlling or improving the behavioural difficulties of their children with fragile X. The behaviours that it has been thought to improve are inattentiveness, restlessness, overactivity, and impulsiveness. Turk concludes that evidence to date shows that regular folic acid may be useful in treating the restlessness and inattention displayed by many children with fragile X, and that further research is necessary to prove this conclusively. It may be that folic acid acts in a similar way to the stimulant medication given to some children who have attention deficits. If that is the case, it may prove to be a useful alternative to some of the more conventional stimulants currently in use. It should be stressed here that the doses of folic acid used in these trials were carefully controlled and it is not advisable for anyone to try over-the-counter preparations of folic acid in an attempt to replicate the results. No medication or food supplement should be given without consulting a doctor.

The other medications that are currently used to treat individuals with ADD or ADHD may also be beneficial for some children with fragile X who display similar symptoms.

The information presented here is summarized from Cooper and Ideus (1996) who write about children with ADD/ADHD.

Stimulant medication has been used to treat the symptoms of AD/HD since 1937. The stimulant, methylphenidate (trade name: Ritalin) came on the market in 1957 and is now the most common one used. In the 1960s and 70s its use became so widespread in the USA that it came under intense scrutiny, making it one of the most well-studied drugs used on children today. It is estimated that 90 per cent of children diagnosed with AD/HD in the USA are on some medication, the majority being on stimulants that work by increasing arousal levels in the central nervous system. It is thought that the symptoms of AD/HD occur due to biochemical disturbances in the normal functions of the brain's frontal lobe. This area is responsible for enabling an individual to attend and concentrate and when it is underactive, the individual finds it very hard to do these things. Stimulant medication acts as a chemical facilitator that raises low levels of activity in this area of the brain, thus enabling the individual to exert the necessary control over his attention processes.

Drugs such as Ritalin, when administered in the morning, have been found to reduce the symptoms of AD/HD and to help a child to attend to his work and regulate his behaviour for typically three to four hours. After this time the effects of the drug wear off and the child returns to his original condition. A second dose may be taken to help the child through afternoon school. For some children, perhaps 20 to 30 per cent, the drug has no apparent effect and is therefore discontinued. Possible side effects include reduced appetite and mild sleep disturbances. There is no evidence to show that children who have taken Ritalin are more likely to become dependent on that or any other drug.

While many people report that Ritalin or similar stimulant drugs have a hugely beneficial effect on the symptoms of AD/HD, they are not a 'cure' for the condition and have no beneficial effects on it in the long term. When the effects of the drug wear off, the child's symptoms return. However, while the symptoms are being alleviated by the drug, increased learning and social gains can occur that can only be beneficial.

Medication is not the only tool to help a child to reduce attention deficits and improve his ability to concentrate. Other interventions can and should be used which are aimed at more permanent behaviour change by helping the child to develop his own strategies for coping with his difficulties. However, there are many people, certainly in America and increasingly in this country, who are turning to stimulant medication as one tool that can help the child to control his symptoms in order to make increased academic and social progress.

Coping with undesirable behaviour in the short term
When a teacher is confronted with a child who behaves in a way that disrupts the normal smooth running of the class and the learning of other children and which is unhelpful to the learning and development of the child himself, she is forced to react to that behaviour in some way to restore order and enable learning to occur once more.

While she may well embark on a longer-term programme to change behaviour, her immediate response, designed to enable normality to be resumed as quickly as possible, is also important.

The strategies found by practising teachers to be most effective in dealing with a child with fragile X after an outburst or temper-tantrum, were:

- To remove the child from the scene of the disturbance, preferably right out of the room or to a place where he feels safe.
- To provide a trusted, familiar adult to talk softly, calmly and reassuringly to the child, staying close but not actually touching the child unless he initiates it.

- To distract the child with a favourite object, toy or activity.
- To allow the child time and freedom to do whatever he needs to restore his own equilibrium.
- As self-control comes closer, to use gentle humour to make the final step to normality.

(Saunders 1997)

Changing behaviour in the longer term

Having identified which aspects of behaviour are undesirable or problematic, and which need to be increased, the teacher must determine the best ways of reducing, eradicating or increasing them. There are many books within the field of education written on behaviour and helping children with difficult or challenging behaviour. It is not the intention of this book to discuss this issue in depth. A brief résumé of basic behavioural techniques will be given, with specific comment on how they might apply or be applied to children with fragile X syndrome.

Behavioural change may be brought about by the consistent application of strategies drawn from behaviourist theory for changing behaviour. They are likely to be familiar to many teachers, particularly those working with children with special needs. They are:

1. Reinforcing desirable behaviour (positive reinforcement).
2. Ignoring undesirable behaviour (extinction).
3. Removing an unpleasant consequence when good behaviour is resumed (negative reinforcement).
4. Punishing undesirable behaviour (punishment).

1. Reinforcing desirable behaviour

In relation to children with fragile X syndrome, reinforcing good behaviour is a powerful strategy. In general, they like to be thought well of and enjoy the positive attention of people who are familiar and important to them. They like to be praised and enjoy the resulting feelings of self-worth. If using praise as the main form of reinforcement, the teacher should be aware of the child's tolerance for attention and keep the praise sufficiently calm and low-key to ensure that it remains pleasurable for the child. If the teacher does not respond appropriately to the child's sensitivity in this area, what is meant to be pleasant for him could become unpleasant and have the effect of a punishment, thus diminishing the likelihood of the desired behaviour being repeated.

Other popular rewards include: time to be in their own 'quiet place'; using favourite toys or equipment; a favourite activity; using the computer; time spent with a favourite person; a letter home to parents; a badge or sticker or certificate etc. The most important factor when using a reward is that it is meaningful to the child. It may well be possible to negotiate rewards with some children, otherwise observation will reveal what is particularly favoured. Whatever reward is used, it should be delivered:

- promptly, so that the child associates the reward with the desired behaviour;
- consistently, so that he knows exactly what behaviour is required to get the reward;
- sufficiently frequently for the child to remember that the good behaviour brings the pleasurable consequence.

These are particularly important with younger or less able children. As the child gets older or more able, or the behaviour gets more established, it is possible to defer the reward, so that the child has to repeat the behaviour on several occasions before getting the reward. Children with fragile X often respond particularly well to visual methods of recording behaviour that show how far away they are from a reward.

For instance, for a child who is interested in trains, an engine could move along a track each time he behaves in the desired way until it gets to the station when he gets to have a ride on a train, visit the station or watch a train video. A child who loves marbles could be given one to put in a clear tube and when the tube is full, he gets to play games on the computer for a whole session.

Thought should also be given to how the reward will be withdrawn after the desired behaviour has been established, e.g. the child may have to wait longer or perform the behaviour for increasingly long times before being rewarded, or they may be happy to transfer the reward to a new behavioural objective. Children with fragile X have long memories for such contracts and may need very gradual weaning off the programme.

A final point to remember is that it is preferable to reward the behaviour not the child, thus depersonalising the behaviour. It is important that the child feels that he is approved of and liked for himself, even though people may not like his behaviour sometimes. Therefore when a child behaves badly, it is preferable to say that you do not like that behaviour rather than not liking the child, e.g. 'That is not a good way to behave' rather than 'You are a naughty boy'. Similarly, when he behaves well it is better to praise the behaviour, 'Well done, you stayed in your seat all through that activity', rather than, 'You have been a good boy this session'. By making a distinction between the child and his behaviour, even the child who has far to go in terms of behaviour can feel valued and approved of personally. This is so important to his self-esteem and feelings of self-worth. The child who feels himself to be a worthy and valued individual is far more likely to have a reason to control his behaviour than the child who feels that nobody likes him anyway.

2. Ignoring bad behaviour

The thinking behind this strategy is that a child may be behaving badly to get attention. The fact that the attention received may be in the form of a reprimand is not relevant as it still constitutes attention. Some children with fragile X may have learned that disruptive behaviours get them attention which they may desire, particularly if they do not get much at other times. There are several important things to remember if using this strategy in the classroom. Firstly, it can only be used for behaviours that *can* be ignored, for example it is possible to ignore calling out but it is not possible to ignore a child who throws a chair at another child. If the teacher begins by ignoring a behaviour and subsequently is forced to react to it because it becomes dangerous or destructive, the child may learn that his behaviour must be more extreme in order to provoke a response. This is the opposite to what is desired.

When a child realises that he is being ignored when he exhibits certain behaviour, he is likely to increase the behaviour in the short term to try to get the attention he wants. It is only when he realises that this is not working that it may reduce. The teacher must be prepared for this initial worsening of the problem.

Other staff and maybe even children must also be encouraged to ignore the behaviour. It will be counterproductive if the teacher ignores it only to have several children in the class drawing the teacher's attention to it constantly.

As the teacher ignores the bad behaviour, she should try to give particular attention to someone who is behaving in a more appropriate way. Using the calling out example, the teacher should state clearly that she is listening to the other child because he put his hand up and waited to be called on before speaking. By doing this, the child has the correct behaviour modelled by the other child and verbally restated by the teacher. He is then reminded how he should behave in order to get attention. As children with fragile X are very good at imitating others, this aspect is particularly important.

Finally, it is important that the child does get plenty of attention when he is behaving appropriately, and that he knows that the teacher likes and is happy to respond to that behaviour. It is too easy in a busy classroom to ignore those children who behave well and focus on those who do not. This must be turned around so that all the children know that appropriate behaviour is responded to.

3. Removing an unpleasant consequence when appropriate behaviour is exhibited

The easiest way to explain this is with an example that might be relevant to children with fragile X.

If the child is misbehaving while seated at his desk during work time, the teacher might fix him with a meaningful, insistent stare. The child with fragile X is likely to find this uncomfortable and unpleasant. When he stops the undesired behaviour, the teacher will avert her gaze, thus removing the unpleasant consequence of the child's inappropriate behaviour.

4. Punishing undesirable behaviour

This is not generally thought to be an advisable technique to be used frequently or extensively. While it may be effective in the short term, one danger is that the child becomes desensitized to punishments so that greater or more severe ones need to be imposed to prevent the behaviour. It also does nothing to teach more appropriate behaviours in place of those that are eliminated, and is not conducive to building up the self-esteem of the child, or a warm, positive relationship between child and teacher. However, if used sparingly, for specific, wilful acts of disobedience that are understood by the child and within his control, punishment can have a part to play in a comprehensive programme of behaviour management. Using an appropriate punishment that neither physically hurts nor humiliates the child in such instances may be considered part of the normal, sensible process of teaching right from wrong.

When using punishment as an occasional method of decreasing undesirable behaviour, it is important that the child knows exactly why he is being punished, i.e. exactly what he has done that is not acceptable. If this is not made explicit, it is possible that the child may wrongly assume that it was a different piece of behaviour that has been disapproved of and then, not only will the punishment have been useless in decreasing the original behaviour, but another, perfectly acceptable one may have been discouraged. It is also important that the child is aware that it is an aspect of his behaviour that has been found unacceptable, not he himself. It cannot be stressed too many times how important it is that the child feels approved of and valued, and that while he may sometimes do something that adults do not approve of and which cause them to administer a punishment, he is still that same worthy child. This is why it is important that punishment only plays a small, specific role within a generally more positive behaviour management regime.

Children with fragile X are usually extremely sensitive children who are acutely aware of other people's attitudes and feelings towards them at any time. Despite being oppositional at times, they generally want to be approved of and enjoy it when their relationship with adults is a positive one. They can get very distressed if they feel that they are not approved of or if they are temporarily in disgrace. For this reason it is preferable that punishments are administered as soon as possible after the misdemeanour and that they are fairly short in duration. It is certainly not desirable that they should drag on over days, e.g. no PE for a week, not only because the child may be overly distressed, but also because they may not remember the original misdemeanour that elicited the punishment.

Self-management training

Wilson *et al.* (1994) describe a system of self-management training which, as the name suggests, helps the child to acquire the skills to manage and control his own behaviour. This is clearly the ultimate aim for all children and the teaching of these skills to children with behavioural difficulties, including those with fragile X, is highly desirable. While it requires a certain level of understanding and the ability to self reflect, which may make it inappropriate for some, it is likely that many children with fragile X would be able to learn and use the technique to great effect.

The authors stress five important considerations when teaching these techniques.

1. To make the child not the teacher the source of the reinforcement. (i.e. the child delivers his own reward or reinforcement).
2. To keep the focus of intervention positive (i.e. the child should work to *do* something rather than *not do* something).
3. The child should set goals for himself rather than have them set for him.
4. The goals should be set and changed incrementally. (i.e. rather than setting the final goal as the behaviour that receives reinforcement, intermediate goals that the child can achieve within a reasonable time-scale should be set, which can be re-set as the child becomes used to achieving his current goal. This can continue until the ultimate goal is reached.)
5. At least one skill or activity that the child can do well should be included in the goals to increase the frequency of the rewards and thus to encourage the child to stay motivated for the whole programme.

The four components of behavioural self-management as described by Wilson *et al.* are goal setting; self-monitoring; self-reinforcement and adjusting goals:

Goal setting
It is important that the child sets his own goals, although it is recognised that many children will need help and guidance to do this. The child's involvement is crucial to ensure that he owns the programme and has a strong interest in achieving the goals set. While it is always important to ensure that goals or objectives are clear and unambiguous, it is even more important in this instance as the child must be completely certain what behaviours are being aimed at and exactly what he has to do to achieve them.

Self-monitoring
As the emphasis is on the child monitoring himself, it is important that the child is able to identify for himself when the target behaviour occurs, rather than him being dependent on the teacher telling him. This may take some time to achieve with the teacher beginning by pointing out each time he performs the target behaviour, moving to a position where she prompts him to identify what he has done when she sees the behaviour, and finally to a point where he can identify it for himself.

When the child does perform the target behaviour he is required to do something to record it, e.g. put a star on his chart, put a counter in a tube, move his rocket one space nearer the moon, etc. It is important that the child is involved in deciding on and making whatever type of recording system is used and that he can put the marks on it himself.

Self-reinforcement

As he identifies that he has behaved in the desired way, the child should be responsible for marking his own chart by himself. It is important that he gets used to delivering his own reinforcement and valuing his own performance. If he is dependent on the teacher pointing out the behaviour, marking the chart or delivering praise every time the behaviour occurs, he is not really learning to self-manage but is being kept at a point of dependency. As the child begins collecting marks on his chart, the teacher or perhaps parent should encourage the child to sit down periodically and review how well he is doing. The child should always be able to see and have access to the chart, but as a step towards self-management he needs to be encouraged to look at it and assess how well he is doing in relation to the tasks set and equate that to an improvement in his behaviour. To start with this may be necessary every day or even more but later this could be every week.

The teacher can comment on how well he is doing and offer praise, indeed this is an essential step towards helping the child to learn how to value his emerging new behaviour, but she should also be aware of the need for the child to value his own judgment of his progress and to learn to enjoy the fact that he is earning his own marks by altering his own behaviour. As the behaviour gradually improves it is likely that external reinforcement in terms of parental, other adult and peer approval and acceptance, will also help to reinforce the improved behaviour.

Adjusting goals

As the original targets are met, the child should be encouraged to reflect on the progress he has made and to adjust or reset his goals as appropriate. This requires that the child can see and interpret the monitoring chart and understand that the marks on it show a significant change in his behaviour. He can then be helped to set new targets to improve it even further.

This strategy of self management described by Wilson *et al.* can be of immense value in helping children with behavioural difficulties to take responsibility for their own behaviour and to learn how to bring about change themselves. The skills of goal setting, self-monitoring, self-reinforcement and goal adjustment are useful skills that can be applied to many areas of life and could be incorporated in the individual programme of many children to good effect.

Specific behaviour management techniques

Finally, a number of specific strategies commonly used in schools today are discussed. These are particularly relevant or useful in the behaviour management of children with fragile X syndrome.

Time Out

This relates to the provision of a specific place that a child can be sent to after an episode of unacceptable behaviour. It can be useful for different reasons.

Firstly, the child can be deprived of the attention of other people, staff or children, which may inadvertently be reinforcing the behaviour. Secondly, by removing the child from the scene of the misdemeanour, the teacher can prevent it from escalating into an incident which could be far worse. Thus, the behaviour is 'nipped in the bud'. Thirdly, the child has an opportunity to 'cool off' and reflect on the causes and consequences of his behaviour. He may be able to do this alone or may need help to do so.

These are all relevant for children with fragile X, but with these children it can also be useful as a place to go to escape excessive stimulation and thus prevent over-arousal. We have discussed how children with fragile X can easily become over-aroused by the plethora of stimuli that exist in the classroom. This can easily lead to a tantrum or outburst if the child cannot control his state of arousal. A safe, quiet and low-distraction area where the child can be sent when he becomes over-aroused or, as he gets older and able to take more responsibility for managing his own behaviour, where he can retreat when he feels himself becoming distressed, is of great use. The provision of such a place, either within the classroom or close to it, is to be recommended in a class that includes a child with fragile X.

Whereas in the past, Time Out was used primarily as a punishment, it is increasingly being seen and used in a more a positive way as described above. It is important when using it with children with fragile X, that the place provided is not seen as a place of punishment, but rather as a place of safety in which he can regain his composure. The ultimate aim of encouraging the child to use it for himself when he feels in danger of becoming over-aroused will not be achieved if it is associated with punishment and having behaved badly.

It is important when using a Time Out room or area, that the child knows why he is being sent or encouraged to go there, what the purpose is of him spending time there, and then that he will be welcomed warmly back into the body of the class when it has served its purpose.

Token economies

Here, the child is given some tangible but essentially valueless item, such as a point, a star, a smiley face etc. when he has behaved in a specified, desirable way. When he has collected a certain number of these 'tokens', he can trade them in for a tangible reward or treat. Children with fragile X often enjoy collecting the tokens and seeing them accumulate, especially if they can be displayed visually in some way. They are also motivated by the promise of a reward, if it is something that is of value to them, and will enjoy working towards it.

When using this strategy it is important:

- to define the behaviour that earns a token clearly for the child so that he knows how to earn it;
- to ensure that the child has to put in an appropriate amount of effort to earn a token, i.e. tokens are not too easy or too difficult to earn;
- to ensure that the amount of time over which they are saved before they can be cashed in is neither too long so that the child loses interest or get discouraged, or too short so that he gets too many rewards and they become valueless.

Calming

While calming techniques may not be so commonly used, they are of particular use with children with fragile X. In Chapter 4 we discussed calming techniques in more detail as we considered how they might be used to prepare a child for work. The specific calming techniques described are of equal value in helping a child with fragile X to reduce their state of arousal when they have become distressed. The important thing is to know which techniques are effective with each child and to use them consistently and for as long as is necessary. Teachers usually become familiar with the methods of calming that work best in different situations and as the child develops, as stated above, it is desirable that he learns how to practise self-calming techniques.

Socialisation

School placement

The issue of placement within an educational setting for boys with fragile X is not easy. While some may be able to cope in a mainstream setting, either with or without help, there are many who need the smaller classes and greater flexibility and expertise of a special unit or a special school setting. One complicating factor is that one boy may have great variability within his abilities. For example, he may appear from formal testing to be in the range of children with severe learning difficulties, yet he may perform in a familiar classroom setting or on practical or concrete tasks more like a child with mild or moderate learning difficulties. Within his cognitive profile he may display only mild difficulties in some areas, such as those involving visual memory, but have considerably more problems in areas requiring abstract reasoning or sequencing. In some settings or under some circumstances his behaviour may be appropriate and controlled and the teacher may only need to make a few minor allowances to accommodate his needs. However, in other circumstances he may display behaviour that would be very hard to contain within a mainstream setting and which requires quite careful structuring of the environment and the day.

We do know that children with fragile X are good at imitating others and that they learn a lot by copying those around them. This is particularly true in terms of speech and language, and behaviour. It is particularly important therefore that they have access to good role models in these areas as not only are they likely to acquire undesirable habits if placed with children with worse speech and behaviour, but they may not have the good role models that would give them positive help in their development.

Consequently, it is not easy to make decisions about placement in a class or school as many needs have to be considered. Of course, children with fragile X vary enormously and for some, a mainstream setting with some help may clearly be most appropriate, whereas for others, a special school may be considered to be the best option. A lot will depend on the nature of the local policies and provision and the resources available and how they are allocated.

When deciding on the school setting in which to place the child with fragile X consideration should be given to his need to mix with same-age peers on a regular basis to give him appropriate role-models. If this means a planned programme of integration from the base of a special unit or school, careful consideration must be given to the type of activity that the child shares with his mainstream peers. Traditionally, the lessons chosen for integration are often those rather less structured ones such as music or art or topic work, to give all the children a chance to work together on a more equal footing, without the emphasis on cognitive skills. Additionally, integration programmes often include a playtime so that the children can mix socially in an informal setting. These may well be the worst times for the child with fragile X to join in with other children. He is likely to find the experience anxiety-provoking, at least at first, as it is a strange environment with unfamiliar routines and expectations. To expect him to cope also in an unstructured setting where there are few routines and where the children are working in groups or as a whole class, is inappropriate. He is more likely to be able to cope with an integration situation where there are clear routines and expectations of the pupils, where the atmosphere is calm and low-key and where he can fit into a fairly formal setting with few surprises. This may require a school to set up an individual integration programme for the child with fragile X on his own, as this type of environment may not meet the needs of the other pupils from the 'special' setting.

The child with fragile X is highly likely to require additional learning support, certainly in a mainstream setting but also possibly in a special setting. Some find it hard to attend to and complete any but the shortest work tasks without help to focus and refocus them on the task in hand. The nature and amount of that support will depend on the child but the school should ensure that sufficient help is available in the class to meet the needs of the child with fragile X without depriving the rest of the pupils.

The class that the child spends most of his working time in should be well-structured, well-ordered and calm, with clearly established, consistent routines and rules.

The class should not contain a high proportion of disruptive pupils.

The class should contain sufficient good role models for language and behaviour.

Ideally there should be space for the provision of a personal area with minimal distractions for the child with fragile X to work in and/or withdraw to.

Most important of all, the child's teacher should be aware of the specific difficulties, needs and strengths of children with fragile X syndrome.

Social skills

Children with fragile X syndrome are usually very sociable people who enjoy the company of others and are keen to mix and make friends. However, their behaviour in social situations does not always reflect this and aspects of their behaviour may not make it easy for them to interact with others or for other people to realise that they are keen to make friends. Their difficulties in making or maintaining eye-contact, being touched or initiating contact, responding to direct questions, feeling relaxed in group situations etc. might make a child or adult think wrongly that they are not interested in making social contact, or that they actually try to avoid it. This could have tragic consequences for the child with fragile X. Many teachers report that before they had a child with fragile X in their class, they had the impression, from seeing them around the school, that they were withdrawn and very much loners. As they got to know an individual child better and built up a relationship with him, they realised how friendly and sociable he really was. Their warmth and sense of humour are often cited as being some of their most endearing attributes.

This highlights the importance not only of including children with fragile X in social activities, but of creating opportunities for them to socialise in situations that will help them to show their sociable side. Schools and classrooms are by their nature social places and the skills that children learn in the classroom and in the wider environment of the school can equip them for the larger social environment outside. Therefore, the teacher should be aware of the extreme social anxiety that children with fragile X can exhibit and the difficulties that they may face in this area, and try to make the classroom environment and the nature of the social interactions that take place there, as stress free as they can.

In the classroom this could include:

- Providing the child with opportunities to work with one other child where they can focus together on a shared task rather than on the personal interaction. Computers can provide a good opportunity for this as the need for eye-contact is replaced by shared focus on the screen.

- Encouraging him to share favourite activities or possessions with another child.
- Considering the composition of any group in which the child is asked to function and avoiding placement with highly disruptive children whom he will find extremely anxiety-provoking.
- Providing good role models from whom the child can learn by imitation.
- Not drawing attention to the child unnecessarily, putting him on the spot or making him the focus of attention within the class, but allowing him to be 'part of the crowd'.
- Not making specific demands on him to perform or do a particular task as part of a large group but letting him know what the task is and letting him join in to the extent that he feels able.
- Not insisting on eye-contact and explaining to other people that not making eye-contact does not mean that this child is not interested.
- Not asking direct questions in front of a group of children.
- Not touching the child unless he initiates it. Children with fragile X can be very physically demonstrative and enjoy cuddles and touch, but generally on their own terms and when they initiate it. This is likely to be with very familiar, trusted people, and teachers often report feeling tremendous elation at being privileged enough to be given a hug, or have a younger child sit on their lap.
- Providing support in social situations that he is known to find hard, for example lunch time in a large dining area, Assembly etc.

Social skills training

Particular skills such as eye-contact and body positioning are crucial to an individual's ability to communicate. The ability to maintain eye-contact and produce a responsive facial expression and body position have been found to be more important than content in maintaining a conversation. (Kelley and Niman 1990, cited in Schopmeyer and Lowe 1992). While people within a school environment may be understanding of a child's difficulties with social skills and may make allowances for them, it is unlikely that beyond school many strangers will do the same. The child who cannot display these skills will be at a severe disadvantage and will find it harder to make and maintain friendships.

Therefore, some thought should be given to the provision of specific training to reduce gaze-aversion and the turning away of the body that is characteristic of many children with fragile X and to help them to develop the necessary skills. This might be part of a speech therapy programme.

Other social skills training that might be offered to young people with learning difficulties to help them rehearse or practise their social behaviour is also likely to be of benefit to the child with fragile X. This traditionally takes the form of role-play within the school and trips out, individually and in small groups, to practise skills in real situations. Children with fragile X often enjoy trips out of school, providing they have advance notice of the outing and know what to expect of it.

Social inclusion

It is increasingly being acknowledged that to be included and valued within the mainstream of society is a basic right of all people. Thankfully, the days of compulsory segregation and exclusion for people with disabilities or learning difficulties are largely behind us. Children with fragile X will enjoy a huge range of social events and activities and it is to be hoped that practical difficulties will not deter teachers or families from including them as much as they wish.

While many families cite limited access and embarrassment at other people's attitudes toward their child's sometimes unorthodox behaviour as factors that might limit their enthusiasm to include their child with fragile X in ordinary social activities, those who do so invariably report that it has been enjoyable and worthwhile. Families also report that the child's own unwillingness to try new activities or allow themselves to be put into new situations can be a stumbling block to social inclusion. However, they also state that if the children are expected to take the step of joining in and are supported as they do so, after a while they become familiar with the new activity and derive much pleasure from it.

Conclusion

It is clear that behaviour and socialisation are inextricably linked. We all need to behave in ways that other people find acceptable in order to be accepted by them and included in social activities. The majority of us get enjoyment and personal fulfilment from being with other people and sharing activities with them. Indeed, for many people, relationships with family and friends are fundamental to quality of life. People who cannot behave in a socially acceptable way might miss out on the pleasure of these interactions and relationships. If they never learn how to make and keep friends or how to join in activities, they may be destined for a life of social isolation. This would be tragic for a child who desired social inclusion but did not know how to achieve it.

Therefore it is crucial that we give high priority in the school curriculum to the development of behavioural and social skills. As teachers we may feel that it is our task to teach academic skills while containing behaviour and leave the issue of behavioural change or development to parents. As teachers of children with special educational needs, in special or mainstream settings, I believe that it is vital that parents and teachers work *together* to address issues of behaviour and social skills, with advice from other professionals as necessary. It is usually the parents along with the rest of the family, and the teacher, with whom the child spends most of his time. It is therefore these people who stand the best chance of bringing about change. It is to be hoped that a common, united and consistent approach will eventually be successful in helping the child to practise acceptable behaviour in every area of his life and learn social skills that enable him to join in and enjoy a wide range of activities. Such a child is likely to know happiness and fulfillment and bring satisfaction and joy to those who share their lives with him.

CHAPTER 6

Understanding the Family with Fragile X

There are many excellent books written about the theory and practice of working with parents of children with special needs. It is not the intention of this book to try to replicate these, but instead to try to give the teacher an insight into the lives of families whose children have fragile X syndrome.

It is all too easy for teachers and those who work in schools to think that the only part of life that really matters for the young people whom we teach is the part spent in school. Of course we know that this is not true and are well aware that not only do 'our' pupils spend more time at home than at school but that most have a huge network of immediate and extended family and friends and a whole wealth of experiences, much of which we know nothing about. If we are working effectively in partnership with the parents of the children whom we teach we may have some insights into a few of the difficulties that they face and may appreciate that it is not always easy for them, with their jobs, other children and own lives, to carry on the rather complex educational programmes that all have agreed are necessary and beneficial. However, it is likely that while we know quite a lot about the medical conditions and the social, behavioural and learning characteristics of the children we teach, and have a wealth of knowledge and experience regarding the teaching and learning process, we know and understand very little about the reality of life with these same children and the joy and heartache, frustration and satisfaction and sheer hard work that makes up life for their families, 24 hours a day, 365 days a year.

In this chapter I hope to help teachers to understand a little of what it is like for a family to live with fragile X syndrome. While it is always true that having a child with physical or learning difficulties will have a profound effect on the whole family, owing to the inherited nature of fragile X, when one member of a family is diagnosed as having the condition, the consequences for all members of the family are even more complex and far-reaching.

Within this chapter we hear the voices of some people who live with fragile X syndrome. They live with it not only because one member of their family has the condition, but because they themselves share the same gene pool and therefore may all be affected by it in one way or another.

It is easy to write about these things in academic terms, to quote statistics and explain rules of inheritance. However, I suggest that this information is of limited use unless it is accompanied by some sense of what that means for real people living real lives.

It is hoped that the people who 'talk' in this chapter will bring fragile X to life in a way that the rest of the book never can, and that as a result, the reader will understand a little of the reality of fragile X. My sincere thanks to the people who have agreed to share their stories.

Receiving a diagnosis

It is sometimes clear that a child has special needs when they are born. At other times it is not until they fail to develop normally that investigations are made that lead to a diagnosis. Sometimes parents have to fight long and hard to get a diagnosis that they feel is the right one for their child. Whatever the situation, receiving a diagnosis is generally traumatic and it takes time for the new knowledge to be understood and assimilated. The advantages and disadvantages of diagnosis in the case of fragile X syndrome were discussed in Chapter 1. It is important for the teacher to be aware of the implications of diagnosing fragile X for the whole family as it is possible that it may be the teacher who first suspects that a child has the condition.

The teacher's role in diagnosis

It can be seen that a diagnosis of fragile X will have major consequences for a child and his immediate and wider family. What then should a teacher do if she suspects that a child in her class who may have previously received no diagnosis, has fragile X syndrome? On the one hand, the teacher has a responsibility to the child and his family to share such suspicions which might be so important to them. On the other hand, the teacher may want to spare the family the trauma and heartache that such a diagnosis might bring, especially if she feels that it could be particularly devastating for them or if she feels that she may be wrong in her suspicions.

There is no easy answer to this. On balance, I feel that a family have a right to a diagnosis for their child's condition if they choose, especially when it has such far-reaching consequences as in the case of fragile X. Therefore to withhold a strongly held view of this kind would not be right.

I would suggest that the class teacher who finds herself in this situation should not rush into anything but should collect as much 'evidence' as possible that would point to a diagnosis of fragile X. Then, if she still feels that her initial suspicions are correct, to seek advice, initially at least, from her head of department and the head teacher, who may be able to consult a professional colleague, e.g. an educational psychologist, who may have more experience of children with this condition and could back up or question the suspicions of the school.

As fragile X is a medical condition the diagnosis can only be made by a medical practitioner. The head of the school may decide that it is most appropriate to invite the parents into the school and tell them that the school suspects that the child may have fragile X syndrome and explain the reasons. It should be stressed that they are only suspicions and that a proper test for the condition would have to be made through the family doctor. The head may suggest that the parents could visit their GP to discuss this possibility. I do not think that it would be appropriate at this early, tentative stage to suggest the consequences for the rest of the family. If the family choose to follow up the school's recommendations and if the diagnosis is positive, trained personnel within the medical field, probably at the genetics centre to which the family is referred should be allocated to deliver the appropriate counselling at each stage. The school staff could try to make themselves aware of developments as they happen and be available to offer support to the family as required. If this is the first time the school has taught a child with fragile X staff could ensure that they are equipped with the necessary information to enable them to make the best possible educational provision for the child.

The personal experience of Judith

Choosing to have a family is such a natural, positive, simple decision isn't it? Of all the experiences we can have in life, few will be more joyous than the birth of a longed-for baby. Our first child, Joseph was born on 24 March 1986 and we adored him. When, during the first 18 months, his development didn't correspond to the baby textbooks, we weren't unduly worried.

Looking back it's tempting to regard that time before diagnosis as a golden moment when everything was possible and life held such promise. But of course life still holds a great deal of promise, it's just that the terms of reference have changed.

There is no good way to break bad news, only the least bad way. I remember standing alone in the kitchen holding on to the telephone like grim death while the consultant paediatrician told me that Joseph had fragile X Syndrome. She was going on holiday and didn't want to delay telling us, but this meant that we had no opportunity to ask questions or obtain information.

But there was no information. All we could find was in scientific journals, full of jargon that we didn't understand. However, it was all we had so we read it anyway.

It was about a month before we had genetic counselling. A month of knowing that our son had some incurable condition but having no understandable information about it and nobody to answer the hundred and one questions that we wanted to ask. (This was in the days before the Fragile X Society was formed by people who had similar experiences.)

When the genetic counselling took place it made up for the rather shaky start. An unhurried consultation followed up by a detailed letter outlining all the facts that we so desperately wanted, in plain English. Then we tried to find out all we could about helping children with fragile X, reasoning that if we could get Joseph the right kind of help early enough, it might make all the difference to his future development.

Looking back, we have no way of knowing whether this made any difference or not, we certainly didn't 'cure' him, but the positive action helped us get through the early months when nothing could take away the yawning emptiness of loss. You feel so cheated, cheated out of the child you've longed for, mourning the death of that child and yet at the same time trying to love and be glad for the child you have. It was like having a funeral for someone who is still alive.

When Joseph was diagnosed in 1987, I was two months pregnant. At that time the gene that causes fragile X had not been identified and there was no DNA testing. I now knew that because I was the mother of an affected son, I had to be a carrier and that I had passed the gene to Joseph. I also knew that my unborn child could also be affected, or be completely normal.

Prenatal testing was not as sophisticated as it is today. I was given excellent counselling and offered foetal blood sampling, an invasive and difficult procedure carried out at 16 weeks which involved taking blood from the developing foetus. I would have to go to a London teaching hospital and it would carry a significant risk of miscarriage. This was a profoundly difficult time for us. Genetic counselling to demystify the science was essential but there was also the human angle. We had one affected child and knew what it meant to ourselves and our family. We knew what reserves of strength we had and how much support or lack of it we could expect from other people. We also knew that our reproductive decision would have repercussions on the next generation. All the knowledge we had went round and round in our heads. It was impossible to make a decision given the emotional condition we were in after Joseph's diagnosis, but a decision was what we had to make.

We made a positive decision to decline the test and continue with the pregnancy. We had a detailed scan to find out the sex of the baby as there was a greater chance of a boy being badly affected. We were having another boy.

Luke was born on 29 January 1988 and spent the first fortnight of his life in special care with a bilateral cleft-palate and breathing difficulties. He was tested for fragile X and found to be positive. He has grown up to be a sunny-natured easy-going child and we love him to bits. We have never regretted our decision.

We had always wanted several children and seriously wanted another. This time we wanted to minimise our chances of having an affected child but that was not easy or simple. We went over and over our options for three years and our deliberations took over our lives even though we determined that they wouldn't. Eventually we were accepted as research patients on the NHS for in vitro-fertilisation (IVF) treatment. Back in 1991 this involved sexing the foetus before it was implanted back into my womb and only implanting those which were female. It may be easy to describe but at the time it was at the forefront of science, highly experimental and with only a very small chance of success. Even if it proved successful, there was still a chance that the child we had could be affected by fragile X, though girls are not usually affected as severely as boys, and our daughter could be a carrier if she was unaffected herself. (It is now possible to screen a foetus for the fragile X gene before implanting it into the mother.) We found it very hard, gruelling, emotionally draining and expensive. As we lived away from London there was a lot of travelling and we had to make ourselves available at weird times of the day or night. As we already had two children, the stress of separation and organising childcare was high, yet we were told that we had to be calm to be in the optimum condition for the treatment to be successful.

The treatment went well and two female embryos were implanted in my womb. I was given a picture of them and we were full of hope. I was quite convinced that everything was going well. I was wrong.

The embryos did not implant and nobody knew why. We were prepared to try again but it was suggested to us that if we waited a few years the procedure might have been improved and this would give us a better chance of success. We began to think 'what if the next attempt fails too? if only we were ten years younger . . . is our biological clock ticking away?' Gradually the realisation dawned that IVF might have been a delaying tactic. The real issue for us was that we wanted another baby and we wanted to get on with our lives so we decided together that we should go ahead and get pregnant by ourselves. We would cope, we would support each other, regardless of the outcome.

I became pregnant. We had done all we could to maximise our chances of having a girl. A friend lent me a book on the subject which had worked for her. We were convinced we were having a girl and names were duly selected.

Jacob was born on 23 November 1994, nearly seven years after his brothers. He was found not to have fragile X.

How can I make sense of all this? One day I was having a really bad day – only just hanging on in there – when someone told me that I always appeared so positive, that I coped so well! My knowledge that I stumble from crisis to crisis in the shambles of my life, always reacting, never in control, was so far removed from their perception that the gap could never be bridged. But I remembered a quotation from Samuel Beckett: 'Ever tried. Ever failed. No matter. Try again. Fail again. Fail better'.

There is some small kernel of stubbornness in the human spirit that will not admit defeat. Bloody-mindedness will see you through and when you can celebrate your different and challenging life – not all the time, but sometimes – well that's a bonus.

Being a carrier

When a child is diagnosed as having fragile X, because it is an inherited condition it must have been passed to the child by one of its parents. This parent is known as a carrier for the condition. With many other inherited conditions, carriers show no effects of the condition themselves, but have a risk of passing it on to one or more of their children. This is not always true with fragile X where the genetics are more complicated. Two facts are of particular significance.

Firstly, it is possible for the gene to be carried and passed from one generation to the next without anyone in the family exhibiting difficulties or knowing that anything is wrong. When a child (usually a boy) is 'suddenly' diagnosed, it is quite possible that nobody else in the family had any idea that the family carries the faulty gene. Secondly, when a boy presents with symptoms and is diagnosed as having fragile X it must be his mother who has passed it to him. Her other children may also have been affected.

It is hard to imagine the shock that a family experiences when they learn that not only do they have one child who has a life-long disability, but that other family members may also have or carry the condition. The mother must face the guilt and anguish of having passed it on to her family and brothers and sisters must face the fact that even if they are unaffected, they face the prospect in adulthood of passing it on to their children. This is particularly acute for girls who are at risk of having a male child with the full syndrome.

Clearly, having the knowledge, there are reproductive options for them. They can:

- have children and accept the consequences of the outcome;
- remain childless;
- adopt;
- have babies through IVF using donor eggs;
- become pregnant and use prenatal techniques to determine whether the child has fragile X or not, then decide whether or not to continue the pregnancy;
- have pre-implantation diagnosis whereby cells from the embryo are examined very early on in the pregnancy and only those found to be free of fragile X are implanted in the womb.

(Carmichel 1997)

This sounds very simple. People who carry the fragile X gene have several options many of which might enable them to have children who are either free from fragile X or only carriers for it. However, when these facts are translated into a human situation the reality of the situation becomes a little clearer.

The personal experience of Linda

I am 26 years old, a full-time teacher of English at a local comprehensive, and married to Chris.

In May 1994 my mother rang to say that my cousin's son had been diagnosed as having fragile X syndrome. Like most people we had never heard of it but my cousin had been in touch with the Fragile X Society and she passed on the information that she had been sent. All the family learnt that they should have genetic counselling as there was a possibility that the gene might be present in other members of the family. Chris and I duly made an appointment at our local genetics centre without really thinking much about it. We had not really grasped the fact that you could carry the faulty gene but be completely unaffected by it yourself. We reasoned that as I was brainy I must be all right. It was my sister who had found learning difficult as a child, perhaps she had it? My sister's result came back first and she did not carry the fragile X gene. We all breathed a sigh of relief and assumed that we were all clear.

My letter came on the 4 January 1995. I was in the throes of a teaching practice in a tough school and I was using all my reserves coping with it. I don't think I took the information in properly when I read that I was a carrier for fragile X, though probably unaffected by it myself. I remember being totally calm about it for a couple of months – we would probably not have children of our own but wouldn't make any decisions until we had been back to the hospital for counselling.

February was a mad month for us. I was still on teaching practice and we moved house as well. Then my sister announced that she was pregnant.

I went to the hospital for the counselling by myself as Chris was tied up with work. We discussed my options regarding children but all I really wanted to know was how my children would be affected if they inherited my gene. The doctors could not tell me for certain but did say that there was a chance that they could have the full syndrome. We talked about my reproductive options and the nurse seemed quite optimistic about them all. I relayed all this to Chris and we began to think about what we might do. We ruled out the option of a donor egg quite early on, even though friends offered their services to provide eggs, as Chris was unsure how he would feel about a child who was not biologically ours. We had heard that pre-implantation diagnosis was a possibility in a London hospital and I think I sort of held that in my mind as the best of the alternatives. The other options remained but we didn't feel too much pressure to make a firm decision yet. Prior to all this I had never given children much thought. All that was for the future.

In September I started my first teaching job and felt OK about the fragile X issue. Then my sister's baby arrived and we went to see him. He was absolutely beautiful and still is. I cried all the way home.

Suddenly I seemed surrounded by people producing healthy babies and it became important for us to decide what we were going to do. I didn't feel that I could get on with my life until I knew what we would do when we wanted to start a family.

We went back to the hospital and enquired about pre-implantation diagnosis only to be told that the London hospital only responded to one enquiry each month. If we wanted to pursue this route we would have to join a very long waiting list and even when we got to the top there was no guarantee that it would be successful. For us this was unacceptable and we ruled it out as an option. I suppose that the reality of our situation hit me then. It had seemed that we had options about having healthy children, but it was looking as though we didn't.

A year from my diagnosis as a carrier I began to think clearly about the options open to us. I didn't know where I stood about the possibility of getting pregnant and terminating the pregnancy if tests showed that the foetus had fragile X. I have a strong Christian faith but felt that surely there are some circumstances when termination is an option. We probably favoured the decision that we would not have children and even began to pick up leaflets about adoption.

In March 1996 it was possible that I was pregnant. I didn't know whether I was happy or sad or whether I wanted to be pregnant or not but I talked to my possible unborn child. When I found that I was not pregnant I knew that I could not leave things to chance any more but had to make a decision one way or another.

On one hand I felt that I was lucky to know about my carrier status so that I could make an informed choice. Many people do not know and have to live with the consequences whatever they are. But the choice was a crushing one and I did not feel able to make it. Sometimes I wished that I had never been tested and had gone ahead and had children without the knowledge of the possible outcome. I felt the pain of having to make a choice and even felt guilty at considering having a child when it could have severe learning difficulties.

Kay helped me to make up my mind. She said that if we really wanted a child we should go ahead and have one and ignore what anyone else thought. If we decided against it I should have a sterilisation so that the decision was irrevocable, or else we would always carry on living with the possibility of children. Before I could make my final decision I had to find out one more thing. I now knew that it was possible to determine my carrier status more precisely and work out the chances of a child of mine being affected, with some more certainty. There was a chance that the risk of my children having the full syndrome would be low. I went back to the hospital for further tests and was finally told that if I had a child there was a reasonable chance that it would have the full effects of the condition. This piece of information answered my questions and ended my soul-searching. I could not knowingly bring a child into the world who might suffer the full effects of fragile X syndrome, and I could not be sure that I could terminate an affected foetus. I decided to seek sterilisation. Through all this my husband Chris was wonderful. We had only been married nine months when fragile X came into our lives, but he told me that he had married me because he loved *me*, not to have children. He has probably not yet dealt with the full impact of never having his own biological children as he has spent the past years helping me come to terms with my feelings about it.

The relief of having made a decision was immense. It took a year and another pregnancy scare before I actually went for the operation as I had to be sure. Finally, it became a way of sealing our commitment to adoption and although it will be a long time before we finally have children, it feels good. If it were not for fragile X, somewhere, some children would have missed out on having two parents who were totally committed to them.

Having a sibling with fragile X

Having a child in the family with severe physical and/or learning difficulties, such as fragile X, will inevitably have an effect on their brothers and sisters. In 1994, the child charity NCH Action for Children undertook a study into the lives of families with a child with such difficulties. They report that nearly 50 per cent of parents who had a child with physical or learning difficulties felt that their other children suffered from lack of parental time and attention.

Most parents in the survey also showed an awareness of the impact of the child with special needs on the daily lives of their brothers and sisters. Examples that they quote include:
- having their toys broken and their games messed up;
- being physically hurt by the child with special needs and younger siblings living in some fear of physical attack. One parent said that she had to lock her other children into their bedroom to play so that they could escape his destructive attacks;
- having difficulty sleeping and being woken frequently in the night because of the special child's inability to sleep;
- feeling embarrassed at the behaviour of the child with special needs in public places;
- reluctance to invite friends home because of their disabled sibling's behaviour.

The survey also found that the activities of the whole family were curtailed by the difficulties of taking out a child with significant physical or behavioural problems and other siblings. One woman quoted described how everything they did had to revolve around their child with difficulties whilst the other children had to take second place.

While most of this paints a rather bleak picture of family life where one member of the family has significant difficulties, several parents also emphasised the positive side of the relationship where siblings showed great love for their brother or sister with special needs and where parents felt that they were more mature, responsible and sensitive to other people because of it.

Meyer and Vadeasy, cited in Carpenter (1998) synthesise a great deal of research concerning the experiences of siblings of children with special needs and describe feelings that are common to many of them. These are:

- *Isolation.* The siblings can feel isolated within the family because they do not have a normal brother or sister to share growing up and the experience of being part of their family. They may also feel isolated from their parents' lives as the parents try to shield the normal child from many of the worries and difficulties of bringing up a child with special needs. They may also feel isolated from their peers, none of whom understand what life is like with a child with special needs in the family.

- *Guilt.* Young siblings may live with the notion that they are in some way responsible for having caused it. They can also feel guilty that they have been spared the condition and are healthy. Leading on from this, as they get older, they also feel guilty that they can go out by themselves, make friends and enjoy a wide social life while their brother or sister does none of these things. Finally, it is also common for siblings to feel guilty when they leave home or go away to study because they are leaving their parents to cope alone with the child with special needs.

- *Resentment.* In many families, siblings can feel resentful of the time and attention that parents are forced to give to the child with special needs, and the fact that the special child appears to 'get away' with behaviour that would not be tolerated from them. Often as they get older they feel ashamed of these feelings, but the resentment can still remain.

- *Perceived pressure to achieve.* Siblings often feel under great pressure to succeed and perform particularly well . They must somehow be the one who never puts a foot wrong and who fulfils all their parents' hopes and dreams.

- *Concerns about the future.* Siblings are frequently concerned about their role in the care of their sibling with special needs when their parents die or become too old to care for him or her any longer.

On the positive side, the authors also describe sibling feelings of:

- *Appreciation.* They can be particularly appreciative of their own health and abilities.

- *Loyalty.* They are frequently loyal to their sibling outside the home even though they may fight with him or her inside it. They are often very good advocates for them, speaking up for them or ensuring that their needs are heard when necessary.

- *Pride.* Siblings see how hard life can be for their brother or sister and therefore feel great pride in the achievements that they do make.
- *Maturity.* Siblings of children with special needs are often more mature than their peers as a result of the particular responsibilities they have experienced and have greater insights into the human condition, making them more empathetic.

The personal experience of Kathryn

Where should I begin?

Should I write about my wonderful mother who managed to stay such a kind, considerate, cheerful person while bringing up a family under such difficult circumstances? Or about my brothers who are real characters but so different? Or how my father has coped looking after my brothers since the death of my mother? Or how I felt at 27 when I discovered I was a fragile X carrier? Or how my husband and I decided not to have a family but then I became pregnant? Or the future and what would happen when my father could no longer manage in his role as carer? Fragile X has been my life. How can I write about these experiences and express myself accurately?

Here goes.

I have two older brothers, Howard and Ian, who are thirteen and three years older than me. I also have a twin sister, Susan. They are all affected by fragile X.

My earliest memory must be of the upset caused when it was suggested that Ian be moved from mainstream education at six or seven years of age. I remember the anguish of my parents when Ian went to a school for children with moderate learning difficulties and shortly after, to a school for children with severe learning difficulties, the same one that Howard, who was sixteen, attended.

I don't know if my parents had any worries about my twin sister, Susan. I remember being put in separate classes at infant school because the teachers felt that she relied on me too much, but I vividly remember the distress and arguments that ensued when the teachers suggested that Susan too should be moved to the school for children with moderate learning difficulties. I think that my father in particular felt that our family had been 'labelled' and were not being given a fair chance. Doctors assured us that it was all a result of either 'bad luck' or 'difficult births'.

It was about this time that I became unhappy at school. Other children would say cruel things about my family. When I was nine I became friendly with another child who was bullied. In her case it was because of recurrent head lice. It was this nine year old girl who first asked if there was something wrong with my parents to cause them to have three children with learning difficulties. It's amazing to think that a little girl could see something that qualified doctors could not or would not see.

During my secondary schooling I started being 'economical with the truth' about my family. It wasn't that I was ashamed of them – just fed up with the lack of understanding shown by others. I remember people staring at them when we were out – Ian has a tendency to hand-flap and bite his hand when excited, and both Howard and Ian 'talk' to themselves. I would stare back at these people until they realised what they were doing, and look away. I now know their reactions were born of ignorance but these were my brothers whom I loved and I didn't want them stared at and mocked.

At eighteen I was due to begin college and train to be a teacher. Like many young adults I had cold feet about leaving home, but mine were because I knew that mum needed me to help at home. However, she insisted that I give it a try and I had a wonderful time and loved my freedom. I knew things were difficult at home and mum missed me a great deal, but she knew I had my own life to live and had to have my chance. Sadly, during my second year of teaching my mother was diagnosed as having leukaemia and she died a few months after I got married.

I believe my childhood was more difficult as a result of fragile X. I grew up in the 1960s and 1970s when there was more ignorance and prejudice concerning people with learning difficulties but there was a unique quality about our family and my close contact with handicap has made me a better adult. I am closer to my brothers and sister than I would be in an ordinary family. I love them dearly and see them as my responsibility for the rest of our lives, but I still wish, as I did as a child, that things had been different.

Helping siblings

It will doubtless put an extra burden on the parents of children with fragile X to consider the extent to which their child with special needs might affect their other children. While some effect is inevitable, as we are all shaped by our experiences of life, most parents will work very hard to try to ensure that the positive effects outweigh the negative ones, at least in the long term.

Meyer and Vadasy (1997) offer advice on the ways in which siblings' needs can best be met and their experiences as siblings made as positive as possible. They recommend that siblings need:

- to be provided with age-appropriate, accurate, easily understandable information about the condition that their sibling suffers from. This must be done frequently as the child matures and can understand more and as advances are made in knowledge about the condition;
- to have opportunities to meet with other siblings of children with special needs, in this case with other children whose brother or sister has fragile X. Also to have plenty of opportunity to mix with normally developing peers;
- to have plenty of opportunity to talk with their parents both about their

experiences as a sibling of a child with special needs and as a child in their own right. Parents should try to set aside some special time on a regular basis to spend with their normally developing children;

- to be acknowledged and responded to appropriately by those service providers who are working with their sibling with special needs;
- to have the reassurance that their parents have made adequate provision for the future of the child with special needs and to know what that provision is.

Being a parent of a child with fragile X

It is probably impossible for anyone who has not experienced it to know or understand what it is like to be the parent of a child with severe learning difficulties. It is certainly beyond the scope of this book to attempt to do so in a few paragraphs. The complexity of thoughts, feelings and emotions defy description and inevitably will change with time.

Having a child with fragile X means having a child with some or perhaps many of the characteristics described in this book. On the positive side, parents of children with fragile X enjoy and celebrate aspects such as:

- the wonderful sense of humour that is enjoyed by the whole family;
- the sweet, loving nature;
- the enjoyment of cuddles from trusted family members;
- their intense enjoyment of favoured activities and events;
- the surprising and often incredibly astute comments and observations on life.
- the unmatchable joy and pride in achievements made;
- the fact that they seem to bring out the best in people who take the time to get to know them well.

However, these must be balanced by difficulties that parents must cope with at home, many of which are unlikely to be mentioned in a book written from a medical or educational perspective. Parents report that these include:

- living with the inconvenience, cost and unpleasantness of incontinence for many years as many are very late to become toilet-trained;
- having disturbed evenings and nights for many years due to their child's difficulties going to sleep and sleeping through the night;
- listening to them say the same thing or ask the same question hundreds if not thousands of times;
- putting up with strange, irritating and persistent noises for hours or days.
- bizarre behaviour that appears to have no function but can disturb the whole household;
- lack of attention skills which mean that they can't settle to an activity for more than a few minutes.

- Wanting or doing everything 'now' because they cannot wait for a second;
- Aggression, sometimes physical, to others, including their brothers and sisters;
- People thinking you are a bad parent because your child looks 'so normal' yet you can't control them;
- Dreading or avoiding even simple outings because of the likelihood of your child throwing a tantrum in public.

In this section, a mother of two boys, one of whom has fragile X syndrome, describes two very ordinary life experiences – a trip to the supermarket and a trip to the swimming pool. The difference between her experience of these events and yours, is fragile X.

The personal experience of Pru

The supermarket

Last weekend both my boys insisted on coming to the supermarket with me – Henry, who's four and has fragile X, because he thinks I'll buy sweets and Lewis who's eight because he thinks that I'll buy him anything he wants with the right amount of pressure. I'm a bit sweaty already, but keep telling myself that it's only the supermarket. I spend the journey telling them what will happen if they don't behave themselves. Lewis looks sullen and Henry, as he does, repeats 'behave selves' maybe 50 times. We get through fruit and veg. without a hitch. The trouble starts when Henry decides we can't have any of the things that I've put in the trolley. He starts shoving them back on the wrong shelves in a fierce temper shouting 'No Mummy' at the top of his voice. Everybody is looking. They think it's funny until they realise that it's not. 'Shall I buy you some sweeties darling' I say softly, tightening my grip on his arm 'No Mummy' he screams.

Lewis is dying of embarrassment by this time and heads off to another aisle. I let Henry sit on the floor and open the packet of biscuits that he's trying to jam between the tins of beans. His distress has reached a pitch that I know from repeated past experience is likely to make him sick and I'd like to ward that off if at all possible.

We head for the check-out leaving aisle No. 42 littered with broken eggs, biscuits crumbs and the odd piece of salami. Oh and two supermarket staff who would call social services if they knew the number, but who clear up the mess instead. I suddenly hear another familiar cry of pain and see Lewis coming towards us holding his head after being hit by a child with a toy machine gun.

By the time we reach the till, Henry can't allow the trolley to be emptied. I try kissing games on the side of his neck while using my free hand to unload. Henry fights back and our 'packer' starts poking him to try to cheer him up as adults do to children who are upset. 'What's the matter with you then? Got out of bed the wrong side today?' If she continues he'll be sick all over her. I fumble for my supermarket 'reward card'. Suddenly I realise that Lewis's head looks decidedly odd and ask him what he's done in the most normal voice that I can muster. 'It's where I got hit with the gun mum, remember?' Oh, yes.

The swimming pool

Henry's leisure time is punctuated by ordinary people doing ordinary things that drive him into a frenzy of frustration. Swimming is a good example. The chaos usually starts in the changing room because no one changes fast enough for him. So while I'm unravelling my tights, he's growling. The noise level rises steadily until he can't hear me saying that if he doesn't stop we'll have to go home. I open the door of the changing cubicle and we are met by a sea of faces. Cautious adults and anxious looking children, I'm not sure whether they're frightened of me or Henry.

Henry throws himself into the water or onto whoever or whatever is in his way. But people often behave unusually in water don't they? Really everything's going swimmingly. The growling has stopped. I can't hear him screaming with excitement because I'm too embarrassed. And he's found himself a little green teddy-bear float. Brilliant. He throws his little body deep down into the water and lies flat, face down, long enough to drown. But Henry's got character so he survives. He hasn't got any sense though and surfaces retching. Keeping his mouth shut is not one of Henry's strengths.

This happy family scene sours as the teddy-bear float drifts away and is snatched by another toddler. Whoops. Henry thinks it's funny because she's bound to give it back. He swims around her thrashing at the teddy, laughing and crying. Now he's thrashing round her doting parents as well and mum and dad close in an attempt to guard the float. 'I'm sorry,' I say to them appealingly, 'he doesn't understand and he just wants his teddy back.' They're sorry that Henry doesn't understand but their little girl has it now and she's not giving it back. Do I say 'He's mentally handicapped. Give it back. She can play with the other three floats'? No, I try other tactics. They all fail. His cheeks swell up. In a matter of seconds his eyes glaze over and I see it coming. 'I'm here', I yell, pulling forward my fabulously cupped navy costume. He gets to me and is sick into it.

We do our best to try to clear up in the public shower at the poolside. Sick floats down the drain and bottles of local authority antiseptic arrive. The swimming party is over.

These events may provide some amusement for the reader as they have been written in a way that invites the reader to see the humourous as well as the heart-rending, frustrating and exhausting side of life with Henry and other children like him. Indeed, a sense of humour is possibly one of the most important attributes that the parents of a child with fragile X must possess. However, when these or similar events are not isolated incidents but the very fabric of life all day, every day, at home as well as on trips out, the strain on parents can be considerable.

What do parents want from teachers?

As teachers we are part of the lives of these parents and others like them. What can we do to help them and make their lives easier? What is our role in the personal drama of their lives? There are no fixed or easy answers to these questions as families have different needs and the needs of each family will change over time according to their individual circumstances and the amount of support that they receive from their family, friends and professionals.

However, it is important to consider what parents might want from teachers and schools that will help them to cope and function better in their task of raising their child. With this knowledge we can begin to see how we can work with families in a way that will be most helpful to them.

From my own work with parents of children with special needs over many years and my own experience as a parent, I have found that parents want and are entitled:

- to be treated as equals in the task of raising and educating their child;
- to be treated with respect;
- to have their superior knowledge of their child acknowledged;
- to have regular interaction regarding their child;
- to be consulted about decisions that affect their child;
- to be listened to and have their views, requests and opinions taken seriously;
- to be kept informed about what happens to their child at school – the small as well as the big things;
- for teachers to have some understanding of the life and circumstances of the whole family;
- for teachers to be realistic in their expectations of what parents can do at home;
- for teachers to acknowledge and appreciate the efforts that parents make;
- for teachers to show their own vulnerability – to admit that they do not know everything and that at times they are unsure what to do and need help.

In conclusion

As teachers we talk very freely these days of 'partnership with parents', knowing that partnership should characterise our relationship with parents and usually having a genuine desire to ensure that it does. However we are not always sure what it really means or how to establish it. While we may feel that we achieve partnership with some parents, there is often a huge gulf between ourselves some of the others, a gulf that comes in part from having little or no real understanding of them or their lives. In this chapter we have tried to do no more than increase teachers' awareness of what life is like for parents and siblings of children with fragile X syndrome and to suggest what it is that parents might want from teachers. It is only when teachers are able to understand and empathise a little with the position of parents that real communication can take place. This chapter provides a starting point, a brief insight, into the lives of some people whose lives are affected by fragile X.

However, all families are unique and those who have shared their lives with us here will be completely different to those that the reader will encounter in his teaching career, though they may well share some similar experiences and problems. If teachers are genuine, as most are, in their desire to work effectively with the parents of the children in their class, they must take the time to understand the unique circumstances of those families. They will then be better placed to see how they as teachers can play a role in helping the child whom they teach to live and function within the family unit in a way that brings gains for the child and the family as a whole. When teachers can approach parents with some degree of understanding of their lives and a genuine desire to help the child to develop within the context of his family and his life at home, true partnership can blossom.

Additional help

Parents and others can get help and on-going support from:
The Fragile X Society
53, Winchelsea Lane
Hastings
East Sussex
TN 35 4LG
Tel: 01424 813147

References

Ayres, A. J. (1979) *Sensory Integration and the Child.* Los Angeles, California: Western Psychological Services.

Bailey, A., Bolton, P., Butler, L. *et al.* (1993) 'Prevalence of the fragile X Anomaly Amongst Autistic Individuals'. *Journal of Child Psychology and Psychiatry* **34**(5) 673–88.

Brown, W., Jenkins, E., Cohen, I., *et al.* (1986) 'Fragile X and Autism: A multi-centre survey', *American Journal of Medical Genetics* **23**, 241–352.

Brown, W. (1990) 'Invited Editorial: Fragile X, Progress towards solving the puzzle.' *American Journal of Human Genetics* **47**, 175–80.

Cohen, I. L., Fisch, G. S., Sudhalter, V. *et al.* (1988) 'Social gaze, social avoidance and repetitive behaviour in fragile X males: a controlled study,' *American Journal on Mental Retardation* **92**, 436–46.

Cooper, P. and Ideus, K. (1996) *Attention Deficit Hyperactivity Disorder – A Practical Guide for Teachers.* London: David Fulton Publishers.

Cornish, K. and Borrill, J. (1999) 'Identifying Neuropsychological Strengths and Weaknesses in Boys and Girls with Fragile X Syndrome.' MHF Briefing 24. London: The Mental Health Foundation.

Cornish, K., Borrill, J. (1999) *Identifying Neuropsychological Strengths and Weaknesses in Boys and Girls with Fragile X Syndrome. MHF Briefing no. 24.* London: The Mental Health Foundation.

Dykens, E. M., Hodapp, R. M. and Leckman, J. F. (1994) *Behaviour and Development in Fragile X Syndrome.* California, USA: Sage Publications.

Fisch, G. (1989) Letter to the Editor: Fragile X and Autism. *Journal of the American Academy of Child and Adult Psychiatry* **28**, 187–93.

Fisher, A.C. (1991) 'Vestibular Proprioceptive Processing and Bilateral Integration and Sequencing Deficits', in Fisher, A. G., Murray, E. A. and Bundy, A. C. *Sensory Integration: Theory and Practice*, 71–107. Philadelphia: F. A. Davies.

Fragile X Society (1996) *Fragile X Syndrome: An Introduction to Educational Needs.* Hastings, UK: The Fragile X Society.

Freund, L. S. (1994) 'Diagnosis and Developmental Issues for Young Children with Fragile X Syndrome', *Infants and Young Children,* **6**(3), 34–45.

Freund, L. S. (1994) 'Diagnosis and Developmental Issues for Young Children with Fragile X Syndrome', *Infants and Young Children* **6**(3), 34–5.

Gibb, C. (1996) 'The Switched Off Gene', *Special Children* **95**, 12–16.

Gillberg, C. and Wahlstrom, J. (1985) 'Chromosome abnormalities in infantile Autism and other childhood psychoses: a population study of 66 cases', *Developmental Medicine and Child Neurology* **27**, 293–304.

Hagerman, R. and Brunschwig, A. (1991) 'Fragile X Syndrome: a clinical perspective'. *Comprehensive Health Care* **1**, 157–76.

Hagerman, R, and Sobesky, W. E. (1989) 'Psychopathology in Fragile X Syndrome', *American Journal of Orthopsychiatry* **59**, 142–52.

Kaufman, A. S. and Kaufman, N. L. (1983) *Kaufman Assessment Battery for Children.* Circle Pines, Minnesota: American Guidance Services.

Kelley, D. and Ninan, M. (1990) 'Communication Skills Affecting Listening Satisfaction'. Paper presented at the annual meeting of the Western Speech and Communication Association. Sacramento, CA, USA.

Kemper, L. B., Hagerman, R. J. Altshul-Stark, D. (1988) 'Cognitive profiles of boys with Fragile X Syndrome', *American Journal of Medical Genetics,* **30**, 191–200.

Kolb, (1984) *Experience and Learning.* Englewood, NJ: Prentice-Hall.

Lubs, H. A. (1969) 'A Marker X Chromosome', *American Journal of Human Genetics* **21**, 231–44.

Martin, J. P. (1943) 'A Pedigree of Mental Defect Showing Sex-linkage', *Journal of Neurology and Psychiatry* **6**, 154–7.

Mazzocco, M. M. M. and O'Connor, R. (1993) 'Fragile X Syndrome: a guide for teachers of young children', *Young Children* (November) 73–77.

McNamara, S. and Moreton, G. (1995) *Changing Behaviour: Teaching children with emotional and behavioural difficulties in primary and secondary classrooms.* London: David Fulton Publishers.

Meyer, D. and Vadasy, P. (1997) 'Meeting the unique concerns of brothers and sisters of children with special needs', in Carpenter, B. (ed.) *Families in context. emerging trends in family support and early intervention,* 62–75. London: David Fulton Publishers.

Miezejeski, C. M. and Hinton, V. J. (1992) 'Fragile X Learning Disability: neurobehavioural research, diagnostic models and treatment options', *International Fragile X Conference Proceedings.* Dillon, CO. Spectra Publishing.

Modell, B. (1992) *Screening for Fragile X Syndrome: A report of a workshop by the medical advisory panel of Mencap.* London: Royal Society of Medicine.

NCH Action for Children (1994) *Unequal Opportunities – Children with Disabilities and their Families Speak out.* London: NCH Action for Children.

Oostra, B. (1998) 'Treatments for Fragile X syndrome'. Unpublished talk given at the Family Conference of the Fragile X Society. Birmingham, June 1998.

Payton, J. B., Steele, M. W., Wenger, S. L. *et al.* (1989) The Fragile X Marker and Autism in Perspective, *Journal of the American Academy of Child and Adolescent Psychiatry,* **28**, 417–21.

Piver, J., Gayle, J., Landa, R. *et al.* (1991) 'The Prevalence of Fragile X in a Sample of Autistic Individuals Diagnosed using a Standardised Interview', *Journal of the American Academy of Child and Adolescent Psychiatry* **30**(5), 825–830.

Reiss, A. L., Aylward, E., Freund, S. F. *et al.* (1991) 'Neuroanatomy of Fragile X Syndrome: the posteria fossa', *Annals of Neurology,* **29**, 26–32.

Saunders, S. (1996) *Fragile X Syndrome: A review of literature.* Oxford: Westminster College.

Saunders, S. (1997) *Teaching Children with Fragile X Syndrome.* Unpublished research paper. Oxford: Westminster College.

Schopmeyer, B. and Lowe, F. (1992) *The Fragile X Child.* San Diego, California: Sinclair Publishing Group.

Slaney, S. F., Wilkie, A. O. M., Hirst, M. C. *et al.* (1995) 'DNA Testing for Fragile X Syndrome in Schools for Children with Learning Difficulties' *Archives of Disease in Childhood,* **72**, 33–37.

Sudhalter, V. (1992) 'The Language System of Males with Fragile X Syndrome', in International Fragile X Conference Proceedings. Dillon, Colorado: Spectra Publishing.

Sudhalter, V. (1995) *Language and Communication, in Fragile X Syndrome: Advances and innovations.* London: St. George's Medical School.

Sutherland, G. (1997) 'Fragile Sites on Human Chromosomes: Demonstration of their Dependence on the Type of Tissue Culture Medium', *Science* **197**, 265–6.

Turk, J. (1992) *Fragile X Syndrome and Folic Acid.* Hastings, UK: The Fragile X Society.

Turk, J. (1997) 'Treatments and Services for Individuals with Fragile X and their Families'. Report of the Talk given at the Fragile X National Family Conference. Hastings, UK: The Fragile X Society.

Turner, G., Till, L., Daniel, A. (1978) 'Marker X Chromosome, Mental Retardation and Macroorchidism', *New England Journal of Medicine* **303**, 662–4.

Verkerk, A. J. M., Pieretti, M., Sutcliffe, J. S. *et al.* (1991) 'Identification of a Gene (FMR 1) Containing a CGG Repeat Coincident with a Breakpoint Cluster Region Exhibiting Length Variation in Fragile X Syndrome'. *Cell* **65**, 905–914.

Westmacott, E. V. S. and Cameron, R. J. (1981) *Behaviour can Change.* London and Basingstoke: Macmillan Educational.

Wilson, P. Stackhouse, T., O'Connor, R. *et al.* (1994) *Issues and Strategies for Educating Children with Fragile X Syndrome.* Colorado: Spectra Publishing.

Index